Allie Esiri read Modern and Medieval Languages at St Catharine's College, Cambridge. An actress from 1989–2000, she appeared in productions from Twelfth Night *for the English Shakespeare Company to* Sharpe's Battle *for ITV, and then worked as a freelance writer for publications including* The New York Times T Magazine. *She is married and has three children (a mini focus group).*

Rachel Kelly was educated at St Paul's Girls' School and then at Oxford University, where she read Modern History. She worked at Vogue *after entering the magazine's Talent Contest and later joined* The Times *in London, where she worked as a journalist for ten years. She is married with five children aged between eight and seventeen and has always loved poetry.*

A Treasury of Poems
for Almost Every Possibility

edited by Allie Esiri & Rachel Kelly

First published in Great Britain in 2012 by Canongate Books Ltd,
14 High Street, Edinburgh EH1 1TE

www.canongate.tv

4

Introductions copyright © Allie Esiri and Rachel Kelly, 2012
Illustrations copyright © Natasha Law

Please see page 276 for poetry acknowledgements

British Library Cataloguing-in-Publication Data
A catalogue record for this book is available on
request from the British Library

ISBN 978 0 85786 557 1

Typeset in Minion Pro and Plebeya Pro
by Sharon McTeir, Creative Publishing Services

Printed in China on acid-free paper by C&C Offset Printing Co., Ltd

Contents

TELL ME A TALE

MAGIC

FRIENDSHIP AND LOVE

ANIMALS, NATURE AND SEASONS

WAR, HISTORY AND DEATH

LESSONS FOR LIFE

BEDTIME

Introduction

'Child! Do not throw this book about; refrain from the unholy pleasure of cutting all the pictures out.'
Hilaire Belloc

An anthology means a gathering of flowers. Unlike the ones you pick from the garden, these won't wither, and will hopefully remain with you.

Poetry was originally oral; it was sung or chanted, passed from person to person, across borders and down the centuries. These days, nursery rhymes and playground chants are still an integral part of a small child's life, but thereafter poetry can all too easily be shunted into the realm of schoolwork or wheeled out like elderly literary relatives at a wedding or a funeral.

Sometimes the poem at a funeral or a wedding manages to 'move the people' (as the great Spanish playwright Lope de Vega said was the job of art). Both of us discovered as children the tingling feeling a poem can bestow. A war poem can have more power than a history book. A love poem has consoled better than a friend. If you want to try a poem as a sticking plaster to help you through a wobbly patch, have a look at our list of poems for possibilities you may be facing, on page 266. The poems in this book are all poems we loved as children, poems we love reading to our children, poems we think you may want to know too.

We launched Britain's first children's poetry app, hoping, in some small way, to introduce poems to a generation of children who were at home with technology and hoped that they would be encouraged to love, learn and even write poems. We made our iF Poems app, and gave them poems to read or hear being read by well-known actors. We hoped they would have fun with poetry in a way they might not have done before.

The response to the iF Poems app was overwhelming. We received emails from all over the world suggesting new poems we might consider. Every day brought a new and often delicious addition to our own library of poetry. We began to gain an increasingly accurate sense of what our fellow poetry enthusiasts believe to be the greatest verses in the English language. Some poems transcend all barriers. These are the poems that everyone loves, the ones that consistently touch the soul. The result has been this book.

In each chapter, we've tried to start with the easier poems, and then move on to some more difficult ones. You may need a dictionary on occasion: some of the language is difficult, but we hope you will enjoy the detective work. We have poets ancient and modern, fusty and frisky, famous and forgotten. We hope we have included a poem for every possibility, almost: as G. K. Chesterton observed, 'Poets have been mysteriously silent on the subject of cheese.'

Peruse, enjoy. It's your book. But don't cut *all* the pictures out . . .

Allie Esiri and Rachel Kelly
London, March 2012

Growing Up

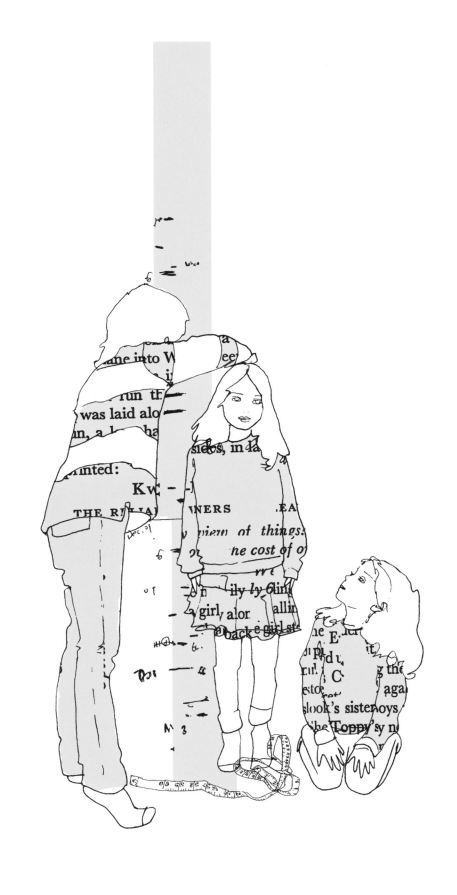

I Want to Know

JOHN DRINKWATER
1882–1937

This amusing poem describes how confusing life can be when you're growing up. Each quatrain, a verse of four lines, is composed of two rhyming couplets, two lines that rhyme. Each verse deals with a different subject and the rhyme is used for comic effect.

I want to know why when I'm late
For school, they get into a state,
But if invited out to tea
I mustn't ever early be.

Why, if I'm eating nice and slow,
It's 'Slow-coach, hurry up, you know!'
But if I'm eating nice and quick,
It's 'Gobble-gobble, you'll be sick!'

Why, when I'm walking in the street
My clothes must always be complete,
While at the seaside I can call
It right with nothing on at all.

Why I must always go to bed
When other people don't instead,
And why I have to say good night
Always before I'm ready, quite.

Why seeds grow up instead of down,
Why six pence isn't half a crown,
Why kittens are so quickly cats,
And why the angels have no hats.

It seems, however hard they try,
That nobody can tell me why,
So I know really, I suppose,
As much as anybody knows.

There Was a Little Girl

H.W. LONGFELLOW
1807–82

There was a little girl,
Who had a little curl,
Right in the middle of her forehead.
When she was good,
She was very good indeed,
But when she was bad she was horrid.

Where Did You Come From, Baby Dear?

GEORGE MACDONALD
1824–1905

George MacDonald is considered to be one of the first writers who aimed to entertain rather than instruct children, and was a great influence on many other poets. As a clergyman, George MacDonald strongly believed in the power and beauty of God's work. This is reflected in this poem, which is in rhyming couplets.

Where did you come from, baby dear?
Out of the everywhere into here.

Where did you get your eyes so blue?
Out of the sky as I came through.

What makes the light in them sparkle and spin?
Some of the starry spikes left in.

Where did you get that little tear?
I found it waiting when I got here.

What makes your forehead so smooth and high?
A soft hand stroked it as I went by.

What makes your cheek like a warm white rose?
I saw something better than anyone knows.

Whence that three-cornered smile of bliss?
Three angels gave me at once a kiss.

Where did you get this pearly ear?
God spoke, and it came out to hear.

Where did you get those arms and hands?
Love made itself into hooks and bands.

Feet, whence did you come, you darling things?
From the same box as the cherubs' wings.

How did they all just come to be you?
God thought about me, and so I grew.

But how did you come to us, you dear?
God thought about you, and so I am here.

The Leader

ROGER MCGOUGH
1937–

I wanna be the leader
I wanna be the leader
Can I be the leader?
Can I? I can?
Promise? Promise?
Yippee, I'm the leader
I'm the leader

OK what shall we do?

My Shadow

ROBERT LOUIS STEVENSON
1850–94

I have a little shadow that goes in and out with me,
    And what can be the use of him is more than I can see.
He is very, very like me from the heels up to the head;
    And I see him jump before me, when I jump into my bed.

The funniest thing about him is the way he likes to grow –
    Not at all like proper children, which is always very slow;
For he sometimes shoots up taller like an India-rubber ball,
    And he sometimes goes so little that there's none of him at all.

He hasn't got a notion of how children ought to play,
    And can only make a fool of me in every sort of way.
He stays so close behind me, he's a coward you can see;
    I'd think shame to stick to nursie as that shadow sticks to me!

One morning, very early, before the sun was up,
    I rose and found the shining dew on every buttercup;
But my lazy little shadow, like an arrant sleepy-head,
    Had stayed at home behind me and was fast asleep in bed.

The Lost Doll

CHARLES KINGSLEY
1819–75

I once had a sweet little doll, dears,
　　The prettiest doll in the world;
Her cheeks were so red and so white, dears,
　　And her hair was so charmingly curled.
But I lost my poor little doll, dears,
　　As I played in the heath one day;
And I cried for her more than a week, dears,
　　But I never could find where she lay.

I found my poor little doll, dears,
　　As I played in the heath one day;
Folks say she is terribly changed, dears,
　　For her paint is all washed away,
And her arms trodden off by the cows, dears,
　　And her hair not the least bit curled;
Yet for old sakes' sake, she is still, dears,
　　The prettiest doll in the world.

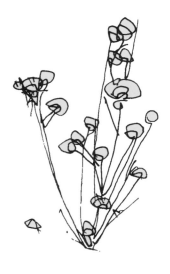

Infant Joy

WILLIAM BLAKE
1757–1827

This poem was published in William Blake's collection Songs of Innocence, *which explores the idea that childhood is a time of freedom and spontaneity. In some of his other poems, William Blake takes a different view, suggesting that the spirit of childhood can be ruined by the rigidity of society.*

'I have no name,
I am but two days old.'
What shall I call thee?
'I happy am,
Joy is my name.'
Sweet joy befall thee!

Pretty joy!
Sweet joy, but two days old.
Sweet Joy I call thee:
Thou dost smile,
I sing the while;
Sweet joy befall thee!

Little Boy Blue

EUGENE FIELD
1850–95

The little toy dog is covered with dust,
    But sturdy and staunch he stands;
And the little toy soldier is red with rust,
    And his musket moulds in his hands.
Time was when the little toy dog was new,
    And the soldier was passing fair;
And that was the time when our Little Boy Blue
    Kissed them and put them there.

'Now, don't you go till I come,' he said,
    'And don't you make any noise!'
So, toddling off to his trundle-bed,
    He dreamt of the pretty toys;
And, as he was dreaming, an angel song
    Awakened our Little Boy Blue –
Oh! the years are many, the years are long,
    But the little toy friends are true!

Ay, faithful to Little Boy Blue they stand,
    Each in the same old place –
Awaiting the touch of a little hand,
    The smile of a little face;
And they wonder, as waiting the long years through
    In the dust of that little chair,
What has become of our Little Boy Blue,
    Since he kissed them and put them there.

Please Mrs Butler

ALLAN AHLBERG
1938–

Is there someone like Derek Drew at your school? Perhaps you behave like him? Does your teacher get as exasperated as Mrs Butler?

Please Mrs Butler
This boy Derek Drew
Keeps copying my work, Miss.
What shall I do?

Go and sit in the hall, dear.
Go and sit in the sink.
Take your books on the roof, my lamb.
Do whatever you think.

Please Mrs Butler
This boy Derek Drew
Keeps taking my rubber, Miss.
What shall I do?

Keep it in your hand, dear.
Hide it up your vest.
Swallow it if you like, my love.
Do what you think best.

Please Mrs Butler
This boy Derek Drew
Keeps calling me rude names, Miss.
What shall I do?

Lock yourself in the cupboard, dear.
Run away to sea.
Do whatever you can, my flower.
But *don't ask me.*

maggie and milly and molly and may

e e cummings
1894–1962

E e cummings was an innovative twentieth-century American poet who created his own poetic style – experimenting with language, sentence structure, punctuation and the visual image of the poem. Notice how he uses lower-case letters and how his use of parentheses (brackets) is not what you expect. The unconventional look of his poems makes the reader slow down and consider all these effects. This was a time when artists were trying new things and changing the way that poems and paintings looked. We could compare e e cummings' work to the painter Picasso's new style of abstract art. For another poem that looks different on the page, have a look at the Apollinaire poem on page 59.

maggie and milly and molly and may
went down to the beach(to play one day)

and maggie discovered a shell that sang
so sweetly she couldn't remember her troubles,and

milly befriended a stranded star
whose rays five languid fingers were;

and molly was chased by a horrible thing
which raced sideways while blowing bubbles:and

may came home with a smooth round stone
as small as a world and as large as alone.

For whatever we lose(like a you or a me)
it's always ourselves we find in the sea

Little Brother's Secret

KATHERINE MANSFIELD
1888–1923

When my birthday was coming
Little Brother had a secret:
He kept it for days and days
And just hummed a little tune when I asked him.
But one night it rained
And I woke up and heard him crying:
Then he told me.
I planted two lumps of sugar in your garden
Because you love it so frightfully
I thought there would be a whole sugar tree for your birthday,
And now it will all be melted.
O, the darling!

Homework! Oh, Homework!

JACK PRELUTSKY
1940–

Homework! Oh, homework!
I hate you! You stink!
I wish I could wash you
away in the sink,
if only a bomb
would explode you to bits.
Homework! Oh, homework!
You're giving me fits.

I'd rather take baths
with a man-eating shark,
or wrestle a lion
alone in the dark,
eat spinach and liver,
pet ten porcupines,
than tackle the homework
my teacher assigns.

Homework! Oh, homework!
You're last on my list,
I simply can't see
why you even exist,
if you just disappeared
it would tickle me pink.
Homework! Oh, homework!
I hate you! You stink!

Love Between Brothers and Sisters

ISAAC WATTS
1674–1748

Isaac Watts is often credited with being the father of the church hymn. His poems were designed to be sung in worship, and include 'Joy to the World', which you may know. This poem encourages us to be kind to our siblings. Watts refers to the biblical story of Cain and Abel, in which Cain, jealous of God's favouring of Abel, kills his brother in order to take his place.

Whatever brawls disturb the street,
　　There should be peace at home;
Where sisters dwell and brothers meet,
　　Quarrels should never come.

Birds in their little nests agree;
　　And 'tis a shameful sight,
When children of one family
　　Fall out, and chide, and fight.

Hard names at first, and threatening words
　　That are but noisy breath,
May grow to clubs and naked swords,
　　To murder and to death.

The devil tempts one mother's son
　　To rage against another,
So wicked *Cain* was hurried on,
　　'Til he had killed his brother.

The wise will let their anger cool
    At least before 'tis night;
But in the bosom of a fool
    It burns 'til morning light.

Pardon, O Lord, our childish rage,
    Our little brawls remove;
That as we grow to riper age,
    Our hearts may all be love.

The Pleiades

AMY LOWELL
1874–1925

The six or seven bright stars known as the Pleiades have long inspired poets. Alfred, Lord Tennyson wrote of the stars, 'Many a night I saw the Pleiades rising thro' the mellow shade/ Glitter like a swarm of fire-flies tangled in a silver braid,' in his poem 'Locksley Hall'. In Greek mythology, these stars represented the seven daughters of the Titan Atlas who holds up the world. The daughters' names are Maia, Electra, Elaeno, Taygeta, Merope, Alcyone and Sterope. They were transformed into the stars to save them from the pursuit of the hunter Orion. Amy Lowell had a particular reason to write about the stars: her brother Percival was an astronomer.

By day you cannot see the sky
For it is up so very high.
You look and look, but it's so blue
That you can never see right through.

But when night comes it is quite plain,
And all the stars are there again.
They seem just like old friends to me,
I've known them all my life you see.

There is the dipper first, and there
Is Cassiopeia in her chair,
Orion's belt, the Milky Way,
And lots I know but cannot say.

One group looks like a swarm of bees,
Papa says they're the Pleiades;
But I think they must be the toy
Of some nice little angel boy.

Perhaps his jackstones which to-day
He has forgot to put away,
And left them lying on the sky
Where he will find them bye and bye.

I wish he'd come and play with me.
We'd have such fun, for it would be
A most unusual thing for boys
To feel that they had stars for toys!

The Children's Hour

H.W. LONGFELLOW
1807–82

ongfellow's three youngest daughters were called Alice, Edith and Allegra, like the girls in the poem, so it is likely that 'The Children's Hour' is autobiographical. Here Longfellow mentions the Bishop of Bingen, a character in an old legend from Germany. The Mouse-Tower is an ancient building on an island in the river Rhine, which is where, it is said, the cruel and tyrannous Bishop died after mistreating the starving peasants of his district, eaten alive at the top of the tower by hundreds of mice. Robert Southey wrote a poem about this, which Longfellow's little girls would have known.

Between the dark and the daylight,
 When the night is beginning to lower,
Comes a pause in the day's occupations,
 That is known as the Children's Hour.

I hear in the chamber above me
 The patter of little feet,
The sound of a door that is opened,
 And voices soft and sweet.

From my study I see in the lamplight,
 Descending the broad hall stair,
Grave Alice, and laughing Allegra,
 And Edith with golden hair.

A whisper, and then a silence:
 Yet I know by their merry eyes
They are plotting and planning together
 To take me by surprise.

A sudden rush from the stairway,
  A sudden raid from the hall!
By three doors left unguarded
  They enter my castle wall!

They climb up into my turret
  O'er the arms and back of my chair;
If I try to escape, they surround me;
  They seem to be everywhere.

They almost devour me with kisses,
  Their arms about me entwine,
Till I think of the Bishop of Bingen
  In his Mouse-Tower on the Rhine!

Do you think, O blue-eyed banditti,
  Because you have scaled the wall,
Such an old mustache as I am
  Is not a match for you all!

I have you fast in my fortress,
  And will not let you depart,
But put you down into the dungeon
  In the round-tower of my heart.

And there will I keep you forever,
  Yes, forever and a day,
Till the walls shall crumble to ruin,
  And moulder in dust away!

The First Tooth

CHARLES AND MARY LAMB
1775–1834 / 1764–1847

SISTER

Through the house what busy joy,
Just because the infant boy
Has a tiny tooth to show!
I have got a double row,
All as white, and all as small;
Yet no one cares for mine at all.
He can say but half a word,
Yet that single sound's preferred
To all the words that I can say
In the longest summer day.
He cannot walk, yet if he put
With mimic motion out his foot,
As if he thought he were advancing,
It's prized more than my best dancing.

BROTHER

Sister, I know you jesting are,
Yet O! of jealousy beware.
If the smallest seed should be
In your mind of jealousy,
It will spring, and it will shoot,
Till it bear the baneful fruit.
I remember you, my dear,
Young as is this infant here.
There was not a tooth of those
Your pretty even ivory rows,
But as anxiously was watched,
Till it burst its shell new hatched,
As if it a Phoenix were,
Or some other wonder rare.
So when you began to walk –
So when you began to talk –
As now, the same encomiums past.
'Tis not fitting this should last
Longer than our infant days;
A child is fed with milk and praise.

It Was Long Ago

ELEANOR FARJEON
1881–1965

Grandparents often want to share trips down memory lane. Although these stories may sometimes seem a little pointless, what matters is not the destination at the end of the journey, but the stroll with a loved one.

I'll tell you, shall I, something I remember?
Something that still means a great deal to me.
It was long ago.

A dusty road in summer I remember,
A mountain, and an old house, and a tree
That stood, you know,

Behind the house. An old woman I remember
In a red shawl with a grey cat on her knee
Humming under a tree.

She seemed the oldest thing I can remember,
But then perhaps I was not more than three.
It was long ago.

I dragged on the dusty road, and I remember
How the old woman looked over the fence at me
And seemed to know

How it felt to be three, and called out, I remember
'Do you like bilberries and cream for tea?'
I went under the tree

And while she hummed, and the cat purred, I remember
How she filled a saucer with berries and cream for me
So long ago,

Such berries and such cream as I remember
I never had seen before, and never see
Today, you know.

And that is almost all I can remember,
The house, the mountain, the grey cat on her knee,
Her red shawl, and the tree,

And the taste of the berries, the feel of the sun I remember,
And the smell of everything that used to be
So long ago,

Till the heat on the road outside again I remember,
And how the long dusty road seemed to have for me
No end, you know.

That is the farthest thing I can remember.
It won't mean much to you. It does to me.
Then I grew up, you see.

I Remember, I Remember

THOMAS HOOD
1799–1845

In this poem Thomas Hood contrasts his youthful, innocent view of the world as a boy with the sadder outlook that has come with age. Though he wrote much serious work, his lighter verse proved more successful and prompted him to comment: 'I have to be a lively Hood if I would earn my livelihood.'

I remember, I remember
The house where I was born,
The little window where the sun
Came peeping in at morn;
He never came a wink too soon
Nor brought too long a day;
But now, I often wish the night
Had borne my breath away.

I remember, I remember
The roses, red and white,
The violets, and the lily cups –
Those flowers made of light!
The lilacs where the robin built,
And where my brother set
The laburnum on his birthday, –
The tree is living yet!

I remember, I remember
Where I was used to swing,
And thought the air must rush as fresh
To swallows on the wing;
My spirit flew in feathers then
That is so heavy now,
The summer pools could hardly cool
The fever on my brow.

I remember, I remember
The fir-trees dark and high;
I used to think their slender tops
Were close against the sky:
It was a childish ignorance,
But now 'tis little joy
To know I'm farther off from Heaven
Than when I was a boy.

All the World's a Stage

WILLIAM SHAKESPEARE
1564–1616

This speech is recited by the character Jaques in Act 2, Scene 7 of As You Like It *and uses the performance of a play and a player (an actor) playing different parts as a metaphor for life. So we progress from childhood to old age, where once again we act as children. And though* As You Like It *is a comedy, this speech has a different, more reflective tone.*

All the world's a stage,
And all the men and women merely players:
They have their exits and their entrances;
And one man in his time plays many parts,
His acts being seven ages. At first the infant,
Mewling and puking in the nurse's arms.
Then the whining school-boy, with his satchel
And shining morning face, creeping like snail
Unwillingly to school. And then the lover,
Sighing like furnace, with a woeful ballad
Made to his mistress' eyebrow. Then a soldier,
Full of strange oaths and bearded like the pard,
Jealous in honour, sudden and quick in quarrel,
Seeking the bubble reputation
Even in the cannon's mouth. And then the justice,
In fair round belly with good capon lined,
With eyes severe and beard of formal cut,
Full of wise saws and modern instances;
And so he plays his part. The sixth age shifts
Into the lean and slipper'd pantaloon,
With spectacles on nose and pouch on side,
His youthful hose, well saved, a world too wide
For his shrunk shank; and his big manly voice,
Turning again toward childish treble, pipes
And whistles in his sound. Last scene of all,
That ends this strange eventful history,
Is second childishness and mere oblivion,
Sans teeth, sans eyes, sans taste, sans everything.

Brother and Sister

LEWIS CARROLL
1832–98

'Sister, sister, go to bed!
Go and rest your weary head.'
Thus the prudent brother said.

'Do you want a battered hide,
Or scratches to your face applied?'
Thus his sister calm replied.

'Sister, do not raise my wrath.
I'd make you into mutton broth
As easily as kill a moth!'

The sister raised her beaming eye
And looked on him indignantly
And sternly answered, 'Only try!'

Off to the cook he quickly ran.
'Dear Cook, please lend a frying-pan
To me as quickly as you can.'

'And wherefore should I lend it you?'
'The reason, Cook, is plain to view.
I wish to make an Irish stew.'

'What meat is in that stew to go?'
'My sister'll be the contents!' 'Oh!'
'You'll lend the pan to me, Cook?' 'No!'

Moral: Never stew your sister.

Humour
and
Nonsense

The Song of Mr Toad

KENNETH GRAHAME
1859–1932

*K*enneth Grahame *wrote* The Wind in the Willows *in 1908 for his son, Alastair. It is thought the inspiration for the wayward character of Toad came from Alastair's naughtiness as a child. The spoilt but charismatic Toad has many adventures, including crashing a motor car, being arrested for theft and driving a runaway train. By the end of the story he is shown the importance of humility by his friends Badger, Ratty and Mole, but this poem shows Toad in the full flush of his pompous glory.*

The world has held great Heroes,
    As history-books have showed;
But never a name to go down to fame
    Compared with that of Toad!

The clever men at Oxford
    Know all that there is to be knowed.
But they none of them know one half as much
    As intelligent Mr Toad!

The animals sat in the Ark and cried,
    Their tears in torrents flowed.
Who was it said, 'There's land ahead?'
    Encouraging Mr Toad!

The Army all saluted
    As they marched along the road.
Was it the King? Or Kitchener?
    No. It was Mr Toad!

The Queen and her Ladies-in-waiting
    Sat at the window and sewed.
She cried, 'Look! who's that *handsome* man?'
    They answered, 'Mr Toad.'

Old Mother Hubbard

SARAH CATHERINE MARTIN
1768–1826

Old Mother Hubbard
Went to the cupboard
To give the poor dog a bone;
When she came there
The cupboard was bare,
And so the poor dog had none.

She went to the baker's
To buy him some bread;
When she came back
The poor dog was dead.

She went to the undertaker's
To buy him a coffin;
When she came back
The dog was laughing.

She took a clean dish
To get him him some tripe;
When she came back
He was smoking his pipe.

She went to the alehouse
To get him some beer;
When she came back
The dog sat in a chair.

She went to the tavern
For white wine and red;
When she came back
The dog stood on his head.

She went to the hatter's
　To buy him a hat;
When she came back
　He was feeding the cat.

She went to the barber's
　To buy him a wig;
When she came back
　He was dancing a jig.

She went to the fruiterer's
　To buy him some fruit;
When she came back
　He was playing the flute.

She went to the tailor's
　To buy him a coat;
When she came back
　He was riding a goat.

She went to the cobbler's
　To buy him some shoes;
When she came back
　He was reading the news.

She went to the sempstress
　To buy him some linen;
When she came back
　The dog was spinning.

She went to the hosier's
　To buy him some hose;
When she came back
　He was dressed in his clothes.

The dame made a curtsy,
　The dog made a bow;
The dame said 'Your servant',
　The dog said 'Bow-wow'.

The King's Breakfast

A.A. MILNE
1882–1956

The King asked
The Queen, and
The Queen asked
The Dairymaid:
'Could we have some butter for
The Royal slice of bread?'
The Queen asked
The Dairymaid,
The Dairymaid
Said, 'Certainly,
I'll go and tell
The cow
Now
Before she goes to bed.'

The Dairymaid
She curtsied,
And went and told
The Alderney:
'Don't forget the butter for
The Royal slice of bread.'
The Alderney
Said sleepily:
'You'd better tell
His Majesty
That many people nowadays
Like marmalade
Instead.'

The Dairymaid
Said, 'Fancy!'
And went to
Her Majesty.
She curtsied to the Queen, and
She turned a little red:
'Excuse me,
Your Majesty,
For taking of
The liberty,
But marmalade is tasty, if
It's very
Thickly
Spread.'

The Queen said
'Oh!'
And went to
His Majesty:
'Talking of the butter for
The Royal slice of bread,
Many people
Think that
Marmalade
Is nicer.
Would you like to try a little
Marmalade
Instead?'

The King said,
'Bother!'
And then he said:
'Oh, deary me!'
The King sobbed: 'Oh, deary me!'
And went back to bed.
'Nobody,'
He whimpered,
'Could call me
A fussy man;

I *only* want
A little bit
Of butter for
My bread!'

The Queen said:
'There, there!'
And went to
The Dairymaid.
The Dairymaid
Said, 'There, there!'
And went to the shed.
The cow said:
'There, there!
I didn't really
Mean it;
Here's milk for his porringer
And butter for his bread.'

The Queen took
The butter
And brought it to
His Majesty;
The King said:
'Butter, eh?'
And bounced out of bed.
'Nobody,' he said,
As he kissed her
Tenderly,
'Nobody,' he said,
As he slid down
The banisters,
'Nobody,
My darling,
Could call me
A fussy man –
BUT
I do like a little bit of butter to my bread!'

Too Many Daves

DR SEUSS

1904–91

What do you think of the series of names that Mrs McCave wishes she had called her sons? We particularly like Marvin O'Gravel Balloon Face – although it might be embarrassing when answering the register at school. Incidentally, Dr Seuss's real name was Theodor Seuss Geisel.

Did I ever tell you that Mrs McCave
Had twenty-three sons and she named them all Dave?
Well, she did. And that wasn't a smart thing to do.
You see, when she wants one and calls out, 'Yoo-Hoo!
Come into the house, Dave!' she doesn't get *one*.
All twenty-three Daves of hers come on the run!
This makes things quite difficult at the McCaves'
As you can imagine, with so many Daves.
And often she wishes that, when they were born,
She had named one of them Bodkin Van Horn
And one of them Hoos-Foos. And one of them Snimm.
And one of them Hot-Shot. And one Sunny Jim.
And one of them Shadrack. And one of them Blinkey.
And one of them Stuffy. And one of them Stinkey.
Another one Putt-Putt. Another one Moon Face.
Another one Marvin O'Gravel Balloon Face.
And one of them Ziggy. And one Soggy Muff.
One Buffalo Bill. And one Biffalo Buff.
And one of them Sneepy. And one Weepy Weed.
And one Paris Garters. And one Harris Tweed.
And one of them Sir Michael Carmichael Zutt
And one of them Oliver Boliver Butt
And one of them Zanzibar Buck-Buck McFate . . .
But she didn't do it. And now it's too late.

Poetry Jump-Up

JOHN AGARD
1949–

Guyana is the only English-speaking country in South America and was a British colony until it gained its independence in 1966. John Agard was born in Guyana; he moved to Britain in the late nineteen seventies and has been having fun teasing the pomposity of the British establishment and the Queen's English ever since.

Tell me if Ah seeing right
Take a look down de street

Words dancin
Words dancin
till dey sweat
words like fishes
jumpin out a net
words wild and free
joinin de poetry revelry
words back to back
words belly to belly

Come on everybody
come and join de poetry band
dis is poetry carnival
dis is poetry bacchanal
when inspiration call
take yu pen in yu hand
if yu don't have a pen
take yu pencil in yu hand
if you don't have a pencil
what the hell
so long de feeling start to swell
just shout de poem out

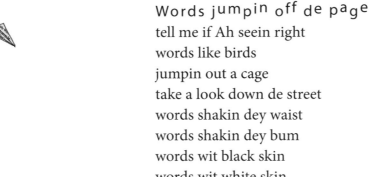

Words jumpin off de page
tell me if Ah seein right
words like birds
jumpin out a cage
take a look down de street
words shakin dey waist
words shakin dey bum
words wit black skin
words wit white skin
words wit brown skin
words wit no skin at all
words huggin up words
an sayin I want to be a poem today
rhyme or no rhyme
I is a poem today
I mean to have a good time

Words feeling hot hot hot
big words feeling hot hot hot
lil words feeling hot hot hot
even sad word cant help
tappin dey toe
to de riddum of de poetry band

Dis is poetry carnival
dis is poetry bacchanal
so come on everybody
join de celebration
all yu need is plenty perspiration
an a little inspiration
plenty perspiration
an a little inspiration

Down Vith Children!

ROALD DAHL
1916–90

Isn't it fun how Roald Dahl plays around with spelling, sqvishing the rules just as the witches sqvish the children? Try reciting it aloud and have fun with all those 'v's! Roald Dahl is one of the greatest children's writers, and his books have been made into films, plays and musicals. This poem appears in his brilliant book The Witches.

'Down vith children! Do them in!
Boil their bones and fry their skin!
Bish them, sqvish them, bash them, mash them!
Brrreak them, shake them, slash them, smash them!
Offer chocs vith magic powder!
Say "Eat up!" then say it louder.
Crrram them full of sticky eats,
Send them home still guzzling sveets.
And in the morning little fools
Go marching off to separate schools.
A girl feels sick and goes all pale.
She yells, "Hey look! I've grrrown a tail!"
A boy who's standing next to her
Screams, "Help! I think I'm grrrowing fur!"
Another shouts, "Vee look like frrreaks!
There's viskers growing on our cheeks!"
A boy who vos extremely tall
Cries out, "Vot's wrong? I'm grrrowing small!"
Four tiny legs begin to sprrrout
From everybody rrround about.
And all at vunce, all in a trrrice,
There are no children! Only MICE!

In every school is mice galore
All rrrunning rrround the school-rrroom floor!
And all the poor demented teachers
Is yelling, "Hey, who are these crrreatures?"
They stand upon the desks and shout,
"Get out, you filthy mice! Get out!
Vill someone fetch some mouse-trrraps, please!
And don't forrrget to bring the cheese!"
Now mouse-trrraps come and every trrrap
Goes *snippy-snip* and *snappy-snap*.
The mouse-trrraps have a powerful spring,
The springs go *crack* and *snap* and *ping*!
Is lovely noise for us to hear!
Is music to a vitch's ear!
Dead mice is every place arrround,
Piled two feet deep upon the grrround,
Vith teachers searching left and rrright,
But not a single child in sight!
The teachers cry, "Vot's going on?
Oh vhere have all the children gone?
Is half-past nine and as a rrrule
They're never late as this for school!"
Poor teachers don't know vot to do.
Some sit and rrread, and just a few
Amuse themselves throughout the day
By sweeping all the mice away.
AND ALL US VITCHES SHOUT HOORAY!'

The Owl and the Pussycat

EDWARD LEAR

1812–88

This nonsense poem makes no literal sense, but it charms adults and children alike with its rhythm, rhyme and ridiculous tale. The repetition of words makes it fun to read and recite. Look out for the 'internal rhyme' – for example, 'honey' and 'money'. The 'runcible spoon' was a phrase made up by Edward Lear in this poem and is most likely a cross between a fork and a spoon.

The Owl and the Pussy-Cat went to sea
    In a beautiful pea-green boat,
They took some honey, and plenty of money,
    Wrapped up in a five pound note.
The Owl looked up to the stars above,
    And sang to a small guitar,
'O lovely Pussy! O Pussy my love,
    What a beautiful Pussy you are,
        You are,
        You are!
What a beautiful Pussy you are!'

Pussy said to the Owl, 'You elegant fowl!
    How charmingly sweet you sing!
O let us be married! too long we have tarried:
    But what shall we do for a ring?'
They sailed away, for a year and a day,
    To the land where the Bong-tree grows
And there in a wood a Piggy-wig stood
    With a ring at the end of his nose,
        His nose,
        His nose,
With a ring at the end of his nose.

'Dear pig, are you willing to sell for one shilling
    Your ring?' Said the Piggy, 'I will.'
So they took it away, and were married next day
    By the Turkey who lives on the hill.
They dined on mince, and slices of quince,
    Which they ate with a runcible spoon;
And hand in hand, on the edge of the sand,
    They danced by the light of the moon,
       The moon,
       The moon,
They danced by the light of the moon.

What is an Epigram?

SAMUEL TAYLOR COLERIDGE
1772–1834

An epigram is a short, witty saying. It comes from the Greek word 'epigramma', which means to write on or inscribe.

What is an Epigram? A dwarfish whole,
Its body brevity, and wit its soul.

Poor Old Lady

ANON

Poor old lady, she swallowed a fly.
I don't know why she swallowed a fly.
Poor old lady, I think she'll die.

Poor old lady, she swallowed a spider.
It squirmed and wriggled and turned inside her.
She swallowed the spider to catch the fly.
I don't know why she swallowed a fly.
Poor old lady, I think she'll die.

Poor old lady, she swallowed a bird.
How absurd! She swallowed a bird.
She swallowed the bird to catch the spider,
She swallowed the spider to catch the fly,
I don't know why she swallowed a fly.
Poor old lady, I think she'll die.

Poor old lady, she swallowed a cat.
Think of that! She swallowed a cat.
She swallowed the cat to catch the bird.
She swallowed the bird to catch the spider.
She swallowed the spider to catch the fly,
I don't know why she swallowed a fly.
Poor old lady, I think she'll die.

Poor old lady, she swallowed a dog.
She went the whole hog when she swallowed the dog.
She swallowed the dog to catch the cat,
She swallowed the cat to catch the bird,
She swallowed the bird to catch the spider.
She swallowed the spider to catch the fly,
I don't know why she swallowed a fly.
Poor old lady, I think she'll die.

Poor old lady, she swallowed a cow.
I don't know how she swallowed a cow.
She swallowed the cow to catch the dog,
She swallowed the dog to catch the cat,
She swallowed the cat to catch the bird,
She swallowed the bird to catch the spider,
She swallowed the spider to catch the fly,
I don't know why she swallowed a fly.
Poor old lady, I think she'll die.

Poor old lady, she swallowed a horse.
She died, of course.

To a Friend in Search of Rural Seclusion

CHRISTOPHER LOGUE
1926–2011

When all else fails,
try Wales.

Dear Mum

BRIAN PATTEN
1946–

Dear Mum,

while you were out
a cup went and broke itself,
a crack appeared in the blue vase
your great-great grandad
brought back from China.
Somehow, without me even turning on the tap,
the sink mysteriously overflowed.
A strange jam-stain,
about the size of a boy's hand,
appeared on the kitchen wall.
I don't think we will ever discover
exactly how the cat
managed to turn on the washer-machine
(specially from inside),
or how Sis's pet rabbit went and mistook
the waste-disposal unit for a burrow.
Also, I know the canary looks grubby,
but it took ages
getting it out of the vacuum cleaner.
I was being good
(honest)
but I think the house is haunted so,
knowing you're going to have a fit,
I've gone over to Gran's for a bit.

Talking Turkeys!!

BENJAMIN ZEPHANIAH
1958–

Be nice to yu turkeys dis christmas
Cos turkeys just wanna hav fun
Turkeys are cool, turkeys are wicked
An every turkey has a Mum.
Be nice to yu turkeys dis christmas,
Don't eat it, keep it alive,
It could be yu mate and not on yu plate
Say, Yo! Turkey I'm on your side.

I got lots of friends who are turkeys
An all of dem fear christmas time,
Dey wanna enjoy it, dey say humans destroyed it
An humans are out of dere mind,
Yeah, I got lots of friends who are turkeys
Dey all hav a right to a life,
Not to be caged up an genetically made up
By any farmer an his wife.

Turkeys just wanna play reggae
Turkeys just wanna hip-hop
Can yu imagine a nice young turkey saying,
'I cannot wait for de chop',
Turkeys like getting presents, dey wanna watch christmas TV,
Turkeys hav brains an turkeys feel pain
In many ways like you an me.

I once knew a turkey called
Turkey
He said 'Benji explain to me please,
Who put de turkey in christmas
An what happens to christmas trees?'
I said 'I am not too sure turkey
But it's nothing to do wid Christ Mass
Humans get greedy an waste more dan need be
An business men mek loadsa cash.'

Be nice to yu turkey dis christmas
Invite dem indoors fe sum greens
Let dem eat cake an let dem partake
In a plate of organic grown beans,
Be nice to yu turkey dis christmas
An spare dem de cut of de knife,
Join Turkeys United an dey'll be delighted
An yu will mek new friends 'FOR LIFE'.

Macavity the Mystery Cat

T. S. ELIOT

1888–1965

T. S. Eliot wrote both serious poetry such as 'The Waste Land' and light-hearted verse such as this poem from his collection Old Possum's Book of Practical Cats. *Here he writes with wit and verve about the mysterious Macavity.*

Macavity's a Mystery Cat: he's called the Hidden Paw –
For he's the master criminal who can defy the Law.
He's the bafflement of Scotland Yard, the Flying Squad's despair:
For when they reach the scene of crime – *Macavity's not there!*

Macavity, Macavity, there's no one like Macavity,
He's broken every human law, he breaks the law of gravity.
His powers of levitation would make a fakir stare,
And when you reach the scene of crime – *Macavity's not there!*
You may seek him in the basement, you may look up in the air –
But I tell you once and once again, *Macavity's not there!*

Macavity's a ginger cat, he's very tall and thin;
You would know him if you saw him, for his eyes are sunken in.
His brow is deeply lined with thought, his head is highly domed;
His coat is dusty from neglect, his whiskers are uncombed.
He sways his head from side to side, with movements like a snake;
And when you think he's half asleep, he's always wide awake.

Macavity, Macavity, there's no one like Macavity,
For he's a fiend in feline shape, a monster of depravity.
You may meet him in a by-street, you may see him in the square –
But when a crime's discovered, then *Macavity's not there!*

He's outwardly respectable. (They say he cheats at cards.)
And his footprints are not found in any file of Scotland Yard's.
And when the larder's looted, or the jewel-case is rifled,
Or when the milk is missing, or another Peke's been stifled,
Or the greenhouse glass is broken, and the trellis past repair –
Ay, there's the wonder of the thing! *Macavity's not there!*

And when the Foreign Office find a Treaty's gone astray,
Or the Admiralty lose some plans and drawings by the way,
There may be a scrap of paper in the hall or on the stair –
But it's useless to investigate – *Macavity's not there!*
And when the loss has been disclosed, the Secret Service say:
'It *must* have been Macavity!' – but he's a mile away.
You'll be sure to find him resting, or a-licking of his thumbs,
Or engaged in doing complicated long division sums.

Macavity, Macavity, there's no one like Macavity,
There never was a Cat of such deceitfulness and suavity.
He always has an alibi, and one or two to spare:
At whatever time the deed took place – MACAVITY WASN'T THERE!
And they say that all the Cats whose wicked deeds are widely known
(I might mention Mungojerrie, I might mention Griddlebone)
Are nothing more than agents for the Cat who all the time
Just controls their operations: the Napoleon of Crime!

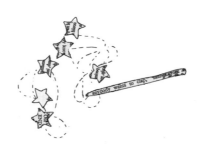

Amelia Mixed the Mustard

A.E. HOUSMAN
1859–1936

Amelia mixed the mustard,
    She mixed it good and thick;
She put it in the custard
    And made her Mother sick,
And showing satisfaction
    By many a loud huzza
'Observe' said she 'the action
    Of mustard on Mamma.'

There was an Old Man on the Border

EDWARD LEAR
1812–88

*L*imericks are fun and sometimes bawdy. They are five lines long and have a strict rhyming scheme whereby the first, second and fifth lines rhyme. They became popular in the nineteenth century thanks to Edward Lear, who wrote his first Book of Nonsense in 1845. Traditionally the first line introduces a person or a place.

There was an Old Man on the Border,
Who lived in the utmost disorder;
    He danced with the cat,
    And made tea in his hat,
Which vexed all the folks on the Border.

The Dong with a Luminous Nose

BY EDWARD LEAR
1812–88

Nonsense poems are not designed to carry a message, but are simply meant to be enjoyed; don't worry if you don't understand what's happening – just have fun with the silliness of the words. In this nonsense poem Lear changes the lengths of the verses and uses an irregular rhyme scheme, so that we never quite know what's coming next.

When awful darkness and silence reign
Over the great Gromboolian plain,
   Through the long, long wintry nights; –
When the angry breakers roar
As they beat on the rocky shore; –
   When Storm-clouds brood on the towering heights
Of the Hills of the Chankly Bore: –

Then, through the vast and gloomy dark,
There moves what seems a fiery spark,
   A lonely spark with silvery rays
   Piercing the coal-black night, –
   A Meteor strange and bright: –
Hither and thither the vision strays,
   A single lurid light.

Slowly it wanders, – pauses, – creeps, –
Anon it sparkles, – flashes and leaps;
And ever as onward it gleaming goes
A light on the Bong-tree stems it throws.
And those who watch at that midnight hour
From Hall or Terrace, or lofty Tower,
Cry, as the wild light passes along, –

'The Dong! – the Dong!
The wandering Dong through the forest goes!
    The Dong! the Dong!
The Dong with a luminous Nose!'

    Long years ago
    The Dong was happy and gay,
Till he fell in love with a Jumbly Girl
    Who came to those shores one day,
For the Jumblies came in a Sieve, they did, –
Landing at eve near the Zemmery Fidd
    Where the Oblong Oysters grow,
    And the rocks are smooth and gray.
And all the woods and the valleys rang
With the Chorus they daily and nightly sang, –
    'Far and few, far and few,
    Are the lands where the Jumblies live;
    Their heads are green, and their hands are blue
    And they went to sea in a sieve.'

Happily, happily passed those days!
    While the cheerful Jumblies staid;
    They danced in circlets all night long,
    To the plaintive pipe of the lively Dong,
        In moonlight, shine, or shade.
For day and night he was always there
By the side of the Jumbly Girl so fair,
With her sky-blue hands, and her sea-green hair,
Till the morning came of that hateful day
When the Jumblies sailed in their Sieve away,
And the Dong was left on the cruel shore
Gazing – gazing for evermore, –
Ever keeping his weary eyes on
That pea-green sail on the far horizon, –
Singing the Jumbly Chorus still
As he sate all day on the grassy hill, –
    'Far and few, far and few,

Are the lands where the Jumblies live;
Their heads are green, and their hands are blue
And they went to sea in a Sieve.'

But when the sun was low in the West,
The Dong arose and said; –
'What little sense I once possessed
Has quite gone out of my head!'
And since that day he wanders still
By lake or forest, marsh and hill,
Singing – 'O somewhere, in valley or plain

Might I find my Jumbly Girl again!
For ever I'll seek by lake and shore
Till I find my Jumbly Girl once more!'

Playing a pipe with silvery squeaks,
Since then his Jumbly Girl he seeks,
And because by night he could not see,
He gathered the bark of the Twangum Tree
On the flowery plain that grows.
And he wove him a wondrous Nose, –
A Nose as strange as a Nose could be!
Of vast proportions and painted red,
And tied with cords to the back of his head.
– In a hollow rounded space it ended
With a luminous lamp within suspended,
All fenced about
With a bandage stout

To prevent the wind from blowing it out; –
And with holes all round to send the light,
In gleaming rays on the dismal night.

And now each night, and all night long,
Over those plains still roams the Dong;
And above the wall of the Chimp and Snipe
You may hear the squeak of his plaintive pipe
While ever he seeks, but seeks in vain

To meet with his Jumbly Girl again;
Lonely and wild – all night he goes, –
The Dong with a luminous Nose!
And all who watch at the midnight hour,
From Hall or Terrace, or lofty Tower,
Cry, as they trace the Meteor bright,
Moving along through the dreary night, –
  'This is the hour when forth he goes,
  The Dong with a luminous Nose!
  Yonder – over the plain he goes,
    He goes!
    He goes;
  The Dong with a luminous Nose!'

Sir Humphry Davy

EDMUND CLERIHEW BENTLEY
1875–1956

This is a clerihew, a funny poem that is four lines long and in which the first two lines rhyme with each other, as do the third and fourth lines. Clerihews were named after the man who invented them, Edmund Clerihew Bentley. Bentley wrote this one when he was just sixteen and sitting in a science lesson at school. The word 'odium' here means 'state of disgrace resulting from detestable behaviour'.

Sir Humphry Davy
Detested gravy.
He lived in the odium
Of having discovered Sodium.

Kenneth
who was too fond of bubble-gum and met an untimely end

WENDY COPE
1925–

This modern poem by Wendy Cope is inspired by an earlier poem by Hilaire Belloc, entitled 'Henry King, who chewed bits of String and was early cut off in Dreadful agonies'. Belloc's poem was part of his series of cautionary tales that include the poem 'Matilda, Who Told Lies and Was Burned to Death' (see page 70). Whether they eat too much bubblegum, eat too much string or tell dreadful lies, all the children in these poems meet untimely ends.

The chief defect of Kenneth Plumb
Was chewing too much bubble-gum.
He chewed away with all his might,
Morning, evening, noon and night.
Even (oh, it makes you weep)
Blowing bubbles in his sleep.
He simply couldn't get enough!
His face was covered with the stuff.
As for his teeth – oh, what a sight!
It was a wonder he could bite.
His loving mother and his dad
Both remonstrated with the lad.
Ken repaid them for the trouble
By blowing yet another bubble.

Twas no joke. It isn't funny
Spending all your pocket money
On the day's supply of gum –
Sometimes Kenny felt quite glum.
As he grew, so did his need –

There seemed no limit to his greed:
At ten he often put away
Ninety seven packs a day.

Then at last he went too far –
Sitting in his father's car,
Stuffing gum without a pause,
Found that he had jammed his jaws.
He nudged his dad and pointed to
The mouthful that he couldn't chew.
'Well, spit it out if you can't chew it!'
Ken shook his head. He couldn't do it.
Before long he began to groan –
The gum was solid as a stone.
Dad took him to a builder's yard;
They couldn't help. It was too hard.
They called a doctor and he said,
'This silly boy will soon be dead.
His mouth's so full of bubble-gum
No nourishment can reach his tum.'

Remember Ken and please do not
Go buying too much you-know-what.

True Wit and A Couplet

ALEXANDER POPE
1688–1744

These are examples of a rhyming couplet. The two lines can stand alone as a poem, or they can form part of a longer poem. The eighteenth-century poet Alexander Pope is famous for his use of the couplet – here are two of our favourites.

True Wit

True Wit is Nature to advantage dress'd;
What oft was thought, but ne'er so well express'd.

A Couplet

I am his Highness's Dog at Kew;
Pray tell me, Sir, whose dog are you?

Fish's Night Song

CHRISTIAN MORGENSTERN
1871–1914

*H*ere are two pattern poems (otherwise known as concrete poems or shape poems).

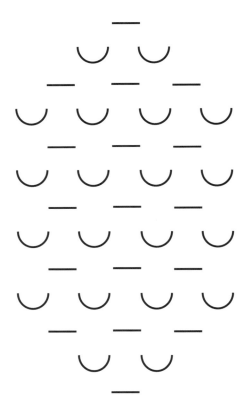

A Calligramme

GUILLAUME APOLLINAIRE
1880–1918

Isn't this fun? Guillaume Apollinaire is probably France's most famous poet of the early twentieth century. He experimented with poetic form. He was also well known for being imprisoned for six days, after being wrongly accused of the theft of the Mona Lisa *in 1916. A friend of the artist Picasso, he made up the word 'Surrealist' and he said of himself, 'Moi aussi je suis peintre' – 'I am also a painter'. He created a book of word drawings – poems which visually imitate their subject matter – and called the book* Calligrammes, *a combination of the words calligraphy and telegram. The Eiffel Tower, at the time of his writing, was used to send telegrams to ships at sea. Here he presents the Eiffel Tower as a symbol of France's might against the Germans.*

The words read 'Salut monde dont je suis la langue éloquente que sa bouche O Paris tire et tirera toujours aux allemands' ('Hello world where I am the eloquent tongue, which Paris will forever stick out at the Germans').

S
A
LUT
M
O N
D E
DONT
JE SUIS
LA LAN
GUE É
LOQUEN
TE QUESA
BOUCHE
O PARIS
TIRE ET TIRERA
TOU   JOURS
AUX   A L
LEM   ANDS

On the Ning Nang Nong

SPIKE MILLIGAN
1918–2002

'*On the Ning Nang Nong' is an excellent tongue twister; try saying it fast and you will tie yourself in knots. Since the words don't mean anything, the way they sound becomes important. Milligan is a master of alliteration ('jibber jabber joo'), onomatopoeia ('Boo!') and humour. He had the last laugh – the words on his gravestone are: 'I told you I was ill.'*

On the Ning Nang Nong
Where the Cows go Bong!
And the Monkeys all say Boo!
There's a Nong Nang Ning
Where the trees go Ping!
And the tea pots Jibber Jabber Joo.
On the Nong Ning Nang
All the mice go Clang!
And you just can't catch 'em when they do!
So it's Ning Nang Nong!
Cows go Bong!
Nong Nang Ning
Trees go Ping!
Nong Ning Nang!
The mice go Clang!
What a noisy place to belong,
Is the Ning Nang Ning Nang Nong!!

The Duel

EUGENE FIELD
1850–95

Gingham is a checked material and calico a kind of heavy cotton. There is also a breed of cat called the calico, which has a white coat spotted with black and orange patches. How do you imagine these sewn toys brought to life?

The gingham dog and the calico cat
    Side by side on the table sat;
T'was half-past twelve, and (what do you think!)
    Nor one nor t'other had slept a wink!
The old Dutch clock and the Chinese plate
    Appeared to know as sure as fate
There was going to be a terrible spat.
    (I wasn't there; I simply state
    What was told to me by the Chinese plate!)

The gingham dog went 'bow-wow-wow!'
    And the calico cat replied 'mee-ow!'
The air was littered, an hour or so,
    With bits of gingham and calico,
While the old Dutch clock in the chimney-place
    Up with its hands before its face,
For it always dreaded a family row!
    (Now mind: I'm only telling you
    What the old Dutch clock declares is true!)

The Chinese plate looked very blue,
And wailed, 'Oh, dear! what shall we do!'
But the gingham dog and the calico cat
Wallowed this way and tumbled that,
Employing every tooth and claw
In the awfullest way you ever saw –
And, oh! how the gingham and calico flew!
   (Don't fancy I exaggerate –
   I got my news from the Chinese plate!)

Next morning, where the two had sat
They found no trace of dog or cat;
And some folks think unto this day
That burglars stole that pair away!
   But the truth about the cat and pup
   Is this: they ate each other up!
Now what do you really think of that!
   (The old Dutch clock it told me so,
   And that is how I came to know.)

Humpty Dumpty's Recitation

LEWIS CARROLL
1832–98

The following poems by Lewis Carroll both appear in Through the Looking Glass, *the sequel to* Alice's Adventures in Wonderland. *Here Humpty Dumpty punctuates his recitation with comments about the way he is behaving and Alice's reactions. Although the words and the story of the poem are virtually meaningless, the way in which Humpty recites it makes Alice see what he wants her to see. Before this recitation Humpty claims, 'When I use a word . . . it means just what I choose it to mean – neither more nor less.' Even Humpty himself is open to interpretation. He is traditionally seen as an egg, because many thought that the nursery rhyme 'Humpty Dumpty sat on a wall . . .' was a riddle about an egg. However, there are many possibilities as to the original meaning of this well-known character's name, including a drink with brandy and a military cannon.*

'As to poetry, you know,' said Humpty Dumpty, stretching out one of his great hands, 'I can repeat poetry as well as other folk, if it comes to that—'

   'Oh, it needn't come to that!' Alice hastily said, hoping to keep him from beginning.

   'The piece I'm going to repeat,' he went on without noticing her remark, 'was written entirely for your amusement.'

   Alice felt that in that case she really ought to listen to it, so she sat down, and said 'Thank you' rather sadly.

> 'In winter, when the fields are white,
> I sing this song for your delight—

only I don't sing it,' he added, as an explanation.

   'I see you don't,' said Alice.

   'If you can see whether I'm singing or not, you're sharper eyes than most.' Humpty Dumpty remarked severely. Alice was silent.

'In spring, when woods are getting green,
I'll try and tell you what I mean.'

'Thank you very much,' said Alice.

'In summer, when the days are long,
Perhaps you'll understand the song:

In autumn, when the leaves are brown,
Take pen and ink, and write it down.'

'I will, if I can remember it so long,' said Alice.
'You needn't go on making remarks like that,' Humpty Dumpty said: 'they're not sensible, and they put me out.'

'I sent a message to the fish:
I told them "This is what I wish."

The little fishes of the sea,
They sent an answer back to me.

The little fishes' answer was
"We cannot do it, Sir, because—"'

'I'm afraid I don't quite understand,' said Alice.
'It gets easier further on,' Humpty Dumpty replied.

'I sent to them again to say
"It will be better to obey."

The fishes answered with a grin,
"Why, what a temper you are in!"

I told them once, I told them twice:
They would not listen to advice.

I took a kettle large and new,
Fit for the deed I had to do.

My heart went hop, my heart went thump;
I filled the kettle at the pump.

Then some one came to me and said,
"The little fishes are in bed."

I said to him, I said it plain,
"Then you must wake them up again."

I said it very loud and clear;
I went and shouted in his ear.'

Humpty Dumpty raised his voice almost to a scream as he repeated this verse, and Alice thought with a shudder, 'I wouldn't have been the messenger for anything!'

'But he was very stiff and proud;
He said "You needn't shout so loud!"

And he was very proud and stiff;
He said "I'd go and wake them, if—"

I took a corkscrew from the shelf:
I went to wake them up myself.

And when I found the door was locked,
I pulled and pushed and knocked.

And when I found the door was shut,
I tried to turn the handle, but—'

There was a long pause.
  'Is that all?' Alice timidly asked.
  'That's all,' said Humpty Dumpty. 'Good-bye.'

Jabberwocky

LEWIS CARROLL
1832–98

Most of the words in this nonsense poem were invented by Lewis Carroll and several have made their way into the dictionary, for example the word 'chortle', which means 'laugh', and may well be a mixture of the words 'chuckle' and 'snort'. Lewis Carroll often combines two words: for example, in the first line the word 'tove' might be a combination of 'dove' and 'toad'. The reaction of most readers is similar to that of Alice, who said, 'It seems to fill my head with ideas – only I don't exactly know what they are!'

It was like this.

JABBERWOCKY

'Twas brillig, and the slithy toves
Did gyre and gimble in the wabe:
All mimsy were the borogoves,
And the mome raths outgrabe.

She puzzled over this for some time, but at last a bright thought struck her. 'Why, it's a Looking-glass book, of course! And, if I hold it up to a glass the words will all go the right way again.'

This was the poem that Alice read:

> 'Twas brillig, and the slithy toves
>   Did gyre and gimble in the wabe:
> All mimsy were the borogoves,
>   And the mome raths outgrabe.
>
> 'Beware the Jabberwock, my son!
>   The jaws that bite, the claws that catch!
> Beware the Jubjub bird, and shun
>   The frumious Bandersnatch!'

He took his vorpal sword in hand:
    Long time the manxome foe he sought –
So rested he by the Tumtum tree,
    And stood awhile in thought.

And, as in uffish thought he stood,
    The Jabberwock, with eyes of flame,
Came whiffling through the tulgey wood,
    And burbled as it came!

One, two! One, two! And through and through
    The vorpal blade went snicker-snack!
He left it dead, and with its head
    He went galumphing back.

'And hast thou slain the Jabberwock?
    Come to my arms, my beamish boy!
O frabjous day! Callooh! Callay!'
    He chortled in his joy.

'Twas brillig, and the slithy toves
    Did gyre and gimble in the wabe:
All mimsy were the borogoves,
    And the mome raths outgrabe.'

'It seems very pretty,' she said when she finished it, 'but it's *rather* hard to understand!' (You see she didn't like to confess, even to herself, that she couldn't make it out at all.)

Tell Me
a Tale

Matilda, Who Told Lies and Was Burned to Death

HILAIRE BELLOC

1870–1953

This cautionary tale describes the sticky end that awaits those who lie. It is humorous and irreverent, a feeling compounded by the dramatic punishment that Matilda receives. Rather as Aesop does in his Fables, *Hilaire Belloc shows the importance of good behaviour, but he adds a dose of exaggeration and humour.*

Matilda told such Dreadful Lies,
It made one Gasp and Stretch one's Eyes;
Her Aunt, who, from her Earliest Youth,
Had kept a Strict Regard for Truth,
Attempted to Believe Matilda:
The effort very nearly killed her,
And would have done so, had not She
Discovered this Infirmity.
For once, towards the Close of Day,
Matilda, growing tired of play,
And finding she was left alone,
Went tiptoe to the Telephone
And summoned the Immediate Aid
Of London's Noble Fire-Brigade.
Within an hour the Gallant Band
Were pouring in on every hand,
From Putney, Hackney Downs, and Bow.
With Courage high and Hearts a-glow,
They galloped, roaring through the Town,
'Matilda's House is Burning Down!'
Inspired by British Cheers and Loud
Proceeding from the Frenzied Crowd,
They ran their ladders through a score

Of windows on the Ball Room Floor;
And took Peculiar Pains to Souse
The Pictures up and down the House,
Until Matilda's Aunt succeeded
In showing them they were not needed;
And even then she had to pay
To get the Men to go away!

It happened that a few Weeks later
Her Aunt was off to the Theatre
To see that Interesting Play
The Second Mrs Tanqueray.
She had refused to take her Niece
To hear this Entertaining Piece:
A Deprivation Just and Wise
To Punish her for Telling Lies.
That Night a Fire *did* break out –
You should have heard Matilda Shout!
You should have heard her Scream and Bawl,
And throw the window up and call
To People passing in the Street –
(The rapidly increasing Heat
Encouraging her to obtain
Their confidence) – but all in vain!
For every time she shouted 'Fire!'
They only answered 'Little Liar'!
And therefore when her Aunt returned,
Matilda, and the House, were Burned.

The Spider and the Fly

MARY HOWITT

1799–1888

'Will you walk into my parlour?' said the Spider to the Fly,
'Tis the prettiest little parlour that ever you did spy;
The way into my parlour is up a winding stair,
And I have many curious things to show you when you are there.'
'Oh no, no,' said the Fly, 'to ask me is in vain;
For who goes up your winding stair can ne'er come down again.'

'I'm sure you must be weary, dear, with soaring up so high;
Will you rest upon my little bed?' said the Spider to the Fly.
'There are pretty curtains drawn around, the sheets are fine and thin;
And if you like to rest awhile, I'll snugly tuck you in!'
'Oh no, no,' said the little Fly, 'for I've often heard it said
They never, never wake again, who sleep upon your bed!'

Said the cunning Spider to the Fly, 'Dear friend, what can I do
To prove that warm affection I've always felt for you?
I have within my pantry good store of all that's nice;
I'm sure you're very welcome – will you please to take a slice?'
'Oh no, no,' said the little Fly, 'kind sir, that cannot be,
I've heard what's in your pantry, and I do not wish to see.'

'Sweet creature,' said the Spider, 'you're witty and you're wise;
How handsome are your gauzy wings, how brilliant are your eyes!
I have a little looking-glass upon my parlour shelf;
If you'll step in a moment, dear, you shall behold yourself.'
'I thank you, gentle sir,' she said, 'for what you're pleased to say;
And bidding good morning now, I'll call another day.'

The Spider turned him round about, and went into his den,
For well he knew the silly Fly would soon come back again;
So he wove a subtle web in a little corner sly,
And set his table ready to dine upon the Fly.
Then he came out to his door again, and merrily did sing,
'Come hither, hither, pretty Fly, with the pearl and silver wing;
Your robes are green and purple, there's a crest upon your head;
Your eyes are like the diamond bright, but mine are as dull as lead.'

Alas, alas! How very soon this silly little Fly,
Hearing his wily, flattering words, came slowly flitting by;
With buzzing wings she hung aloft, then near and nearer drew,
Thinking only of her brilliant eyes, and green and purple hue;
Thinking only of her crested head – poor foolish thing! At last,
Up jumped the cunning Spider, and fiercely held her fast.
He dragged her up his winding stair, into his dismal den
Within his little parlour – but she ne'er came out again!

And now, dear little children, who may this story read,
To idle, silly, flattering words, I pray you ne'er give heed;
Unto an evil counsellor close heart, and ear, and eye,
And take a lesson from this tale of the Spider and the Fly.

The Pied Piper of Hamelin

BY ROBERT BROWNING
1812–89

The story of the Pied Piper stems from the Middle Ages and is based on a real event long ago when the children of Hamelin in Germany really did disappear. The figure of the Pied Piper may represent a plague that led to the children's deaths. A stained-glass window portraying the tale was installed in the church of Hamelin around 1300, and, in the centuries that followed, the Pied Piper story was retold by many writers, from the Brothers Grimm to Goethe. The last verse addresses 'Willy', the son of a friend for whom Robert Browning wrote the poem.

Hamelin Town's in Brunswick,
　　By famous Hanover city;
The river Weser, deep and wide,
Washes its wall on the southern side;
A pleasanter spot you never spied;
　　But, when begins my ditty,
Almost five hundred years ago,
To see the townsfolk suffer so
　　From vermin, was a pity.

　　Rats!
They fought the dogs, and killed the cats,
　　And bit the babies in the cradles,
And ate the cheeses out of the vats,
　　And licked the soup from the cooks' own ladles,
Split open the kegs of salted sprats,
Made nests inside men's Sunday hats,
And even spoiled the women's chats,
　　　　By drowning their speaking
　　　　With shrieking and squeaking
In fifty different sharps and flats.

At last the people in a body
	To the Town Hall came flocking:
''Tis clear,' cried they, 'our Mayor's a noddy;
	And as for our Corporation – shocking
To think we buy gowns lined with ermine
For dolts that can't or won't determine
What's best to rid us of our vermin!
You hope, because you're old and obese,
To find in the furry civic robe ease?
Rouse up, Sirs! Give your brains a racking
To find the remedy we're lacking,
Or, sure as fate, we'll send you packing!'
At this the Mayor and Corporation
Quaked with a mighty consternation.

An hour they sate in council,
	At length the Mayor broke silence:
'For a guilder I'd my ermine gown sell;
	I wish I were a mile hence!
It's easy to bid one rack one's brain –
I'm sure my poor head aches again,
I've scratched it so, and all in vain.
Oh for a trap, a trap, a trap!'
Just as he said this, what should hap
At the chamber door but a gentle tap?
'Bless us,' cried the Mayor, 'what's that?'
(With the Corporation as he sat,
Looking little though wondrous fat;
Nor brighter was his eye, nor moister
Than a too-long-opened oyster,
Save when at noon his paunch grew mutinous
For a plate of turtle green and glutinous)
'Only a scraping of shoes on the mat?
Anything like the sound of a rat
Makes my heart go pit-a-pat!'

'Come in!' the Mayor cried, looking bigger:
And in did come the strangest figure!
His queer long coat from heel to head
Was half of yellow and half of red;
And he himself was tall and thin,
With sharp blue eyes, each like a pin,
And light loose hair, yet swarthy skin,
No tuft on cheek nor beard on chin,
But lips where smiles went out and in;
There was no guessing his kith and kin:
And nobody could enough admire
The tall man and his quaint attire.
Quoth one: 'It's as my great-grandsire,
Starting up at the Trump of Doom's tone,
Had walked this way from his painted tombstone!'

He advanced to the council-table:
And, 'Please your honours,' said he, 'I'm able,
By means of a secret charm, to draw
    All creatures living beneath the sun,
    That creep or swim or fly or run,
After me so as you never saw!
And I chiefly use my charm
On creatures that do people harm,
The mole and toad and newt and viper;
And people call me the Pied Piper.'
(And here they noticed round his neck
    A scarf of red and yellow stripe,
To match with his coat of the selfsame cheque;
    And at the scarf's end hung a pipe;
And his fingers, they noticed, were ever straying
As if impatient to be playing
Upon this pipe, as low it dangled
Over his vesture so old-fangled.)
'Yet,' said he, 'poor piper as I am,
In Tartary I freed the Cham,
    Last June, from his huge swarms of gnats;

I eased in Asia the Nizam
   Of a monstrous brood of vampire-bats;
And as for what your brain bewilders,
   If I can rid your town of rats
Will you give me a thousand guilders?'
'One? fifty thousand!' – was the exclamation
Of the astonished Mayor and Corporation.

Into the street the Piper stepped,
   Smiling first a little smile,
As if he knew what magic slept
   In his quiet pipe the while;
Then, like a musical adept,
To blow the pipe his lips he wrinkled,
And green and blue his sharp eyes twinkled
Like a candle flame where salt is sprinkled;
And ere three shrill notes the pipe uttered,
You heard as if an army muttered;
And the muttering grew to a grumbling;
And the grumbling grew to a mighty rumbling;
And out of the houses the rats came tumbling.
Great rats, small rats, lean rats, brawny rats,
Brown rats, black rats, grey rats, tawny rats,
Grave old plodders, gay young friskers,
   Fathers, mothers, uncles, cousins,
Cocking tails and pricking whiskers,
   Families by tens and dozens,
Brothers, sisters, husbands, wives –
Followed the Piper for their lives.
From street to street he piped advancing,
And step for step they followed dancing,
Until they came to the river Weser,
   Wherein all plunged and perished!
– Save one who, stout as Julius Caesar,
Swam across and lived to carry
   (As he, the manuscript he cherished)
To Rat-land home his commentary:

Which was, 'At the first shrill notes of the pipe
I heard a sound as of scraping tripe,
And putting apples, wondrous ripe,
Into a cider-press's gripe:
And a moving away of pickle-tub-boards,
And a leaving ajar of conserve-cupboards,
And a drawing the corks of train-oil-flasks,
And a breaking the hoops of butter-casks;
And it seemed as if a voice
   (Sweeter far than by harp or by psaltery
Is breathed) called out "Oh, rats, rejoice!
   The world is grown to one vast drysaltery!
So munch on, crunch on, take your nuncheon,
Breakfast, supper, dinner, luncheon!"
And just as a bulky sugar-puncheon,
All ready staved, like a great sun shone
Glorious scarce an inch before me,
Just as methought it said "Come, bore me!"
– I found the Weser rolling o'er me.'

You should have heard the Hamelin people
Ringing the bells till they rocked the steeple.
'Go,' cried the Mayor, 'and get long poles,
Poke out the nests and block up the holes!
Consult with carpenters and builders,
And leave in our town not even a trace
Of the rats!' – when suddenly, up the face
Of the Piper perked in the market-place,
With a, 'First, if you please, my thousand guilders!'

A thousand guilders! The Mayor looked blue;
So did the Corporation too.
For council dinners made rare havoc
With Claret, Moselle, Vin-de-Grave, Hock;
And half the money would replenish
Their cellar's biggest butt with Rhenish.
To pay this sum to a wandering fellow

be grilled

With a gypsy coat of red and yellow!
'Beside,' quoth the Mayor with a knowing wink,
'Our business was done at the river's brink;
We saw with our eyes the vermin sink,
And what's dead can't come to life, I think.
So, friend, we're not the folks to shrink
From the duty of giving you something for drink,
And a matter of money to put in your poke;
But, as for the guilders, what we spoke
Of them, as you very well know, was in joke.
Beside, our losses have made us thrifty.
A thousand guilders! Come, take fifty!'

The Piper's face fell, and he cried
'No trifling! I can't wait, beside!
I've promised to visit by dinnertime
Bagdat, and accept the prime
Of the Head Cook's pottage, all he's rich in,
For having left, in the Caliph's kitchen,
Of a nest of scorpions no survivor
With him I proved no bargain-driver,
With you, don't think I'll bate a stiver!
And folks who put me in a passion
May find me pipe after another fashion.'

'How?' cried the Mayor, 'd'ye think I'll brook
Being worse treated than a Cook?
Insulted by a lazy ribald
With idle pipe and vesture piebald?
You threaten us, fellow? Do your worst,
Blow your pipe there till you burst!'

Once more he stepped into the street;
    And to his lips again
    Laid his long pipe of smooth straight cane;
And ere he blew three notes (such sweet
Soft notes as yet musician's cunning
    Never gave the enraptured air)

There was a rustling, that seemed like a bustling
Of merry crowds justling at pitching and hustling,
Small feet were pattering, wooden shoes clattering,
Little hands clapping and little tongues chattering,
And, like fowls in a farmyard when barley is scattering,
Out came the children running.

All the little boys and girls,
With rosy cheeks and flaxen curls,
And sparkling eyes and teeth like pearls,
Tripping and skipping, ran merrily after
The wonderful music with shouting and laughter.

The Mayor was dumb, and the Council stood
As if they were changed into blocks of wood,
Unable to move a step, or cry
To the children merrily skipping by
And could only follow with the eye
That joyous crowd at the Piper's back.
But how the Mayor was on the rack,
And the wretched Council's bosoms beat,
As the Piper turned from the High Street
To where the Weser rolled its waters
Right in the way of their sons and daughters!
However he turned from South to West,
And to Koppelberg Hill his steps addressed,
And after him the children pressed;
Great was the joy in every breast.
'He never can cross that mighty top!
He's forced to let the piping drop,
And we shall see our children stop!'
When, lo, as they reached the mountain's side,
A wondrous portal opened wide,
As if a cavern was suddenly hollowed;
And the Piper advanced and the children followed,
And when all were in to the very last,
The door in the mountain-side shut fast.
Did I say, all? No! One was lame,

And could not dance the whole of the way;
And in after years, if you would blame
　　His sadness, he was used to say,
'It's dull in our town since my playmates left!
I can't forget that I'm bereft
Of all the pleasant sights they see,
Which the Piper also promised me:
For he led us, he said, to a joyous land,

Joining the town and just at hand,
Where waters gushed and fruit-trees grew,
And flowers put forth a fairer hue,
And everything was strange and new;
The sparrows were brighter than peacocks here,
And their dogs outran our fallow deer,
And honey-bees had lost their stings,
And horses were born with eagles' wings:
And just as I became assured
My lame foot would be speedily cured,
The music stopped and I stood still,
And found myself outside the hill,
Left alone against my will,
To go now limping as before,
And never hear of that country more!'

Alas, alas for Hamelin!
　　There came into many a burgher's pate
　　A text which says, that heaven's gate
　　Opes to the rich at as easy rate
As the needle's eye takes a camel in!
The Mayor sent East, West, North and South,
To offer the Piper, by word of mouth,
　　Wherever it was men's lot to find him,
Silver and gold to his heart's content,
If he'd only return the way he went,
　　And bring the children behind him.
But when they saw 'twas a lost endeavour,
And Piper and dancers were gone for ever,

They made a decree that lawyers never
    Should think their records dated duly
If, after the day of the month and year,
These words did not as well appear,
'And so long after what happened here
    On the Twenty-second of July,
Thirteen hundred and seventy-six:'
And the better in memory to fix
The place of the children's last retreat,
They called it, the Pied Piper's Street –
Where any one playing on pipe or tabor
Was sure for the future to lose his labour.
Nor suffered they hostelry or tavern
    To shock with mirth a street so solemn;
But opposite the place of the cavern
    They wrote the story on a column,
And on the great church-window painted
The same, to make the world acquainted
How their children were stolen away,
And there it stands to this very day.
And I must not omit to say
That in Transylvania there's a tribe
Of alien people who ascribe
The outlandish ways and dress
On which their neighbours lay such stress,
To their fathers and mothers having risen
Out of some subterraneous prison
Into which they were trepanned
Long time ago in a mighty band
Out of Hamelin town in Brunswick land,
But how or why, they don't understand.

So, Willy, let you and me be wipers
Of scores out with all men – especially pipers!
And, whether they pipe us free, from rats or from mice,
If we've promised them aught, let us keep our promise.

The Little Dog's Day

RUPERT BROOKE
1887–1915

All in the town were still asleep,
When the sun came up with a shout and a leap.
In the lonely streets unseen by man,
A little dog danced. And the day began.

All his life he'd been good, as far as he could,
And the poor little beast had done all that he should.
But this morning he swore, by Odin and Thor
And the Canine Valhalla – he'd stand it no more!

So his prayer he got granted – to do just what he wanted,
Prevented by none, for the space of one day.
'Jam incipiebo, sedere facebo,'
In dog-Latin he quoth, *'Euge! sophos! hurray!'*

He fought with the he-dogs, and winked at the she-dogs,
A thing that had never been *heard* of before.
'For the stigma of gluttony, I care not a button!' he
Cried, and ate all he could swallow – and more.

He took sinewy lumps from the shins of old frumps,
And mangled the errand-boys – when he could get 'em.
He shammed furious rabies, and bit all the babies,
And followed the cats up the trees, and then ate 'em!'

They thought 'twas the devil was holding a revel,
And sent for the parson to drive him away;
For the town never knew such a hullabaloo
As that little dog raised – till the end of that day.

When the blood-red sun had gone burning down,
And the lights were lit in the little town,
Outside, in the gloom of the twilight grey,
The little dog died when he'd had his day.

A Smuggler's Song

RUDYARD KIPLING
1865–1936

This poem describes the smuggling trade that was rife in the eighteenth century. Smugglers brought luxury goods such as brandy, tobacco and lace secretly into the country to avoid import tax. It is told in the voice of the smuggler, making it a 'persona' poem or a 'dramatic monologue'. This poem is often sung.

If you wake at midnight, and hear a horse's feet,
Don't go drawing back the blind, or looking in the street.
Them that ask no questions isn't told a lie.
Watch the wall, my darling, while the Gentlemen go by!
 Five and twenty ponies,
 Trotting through the dark –
 Brandy for the Parson,
 'Baccy for the Clerk;
 Laces for a lady, letters for a spy,
And watch the wall, my darling, while the Gentlemen go by!

Running round the woodlump if you chance to find
Little barrels, roped and tarred, all full of brandy-wine,
Don't you shout to come and look, nor use 'em for your play.
Put the brishwood back again – and they'll be gone next day!

If you see the stable-door setting open wide;
If you see a tired horse lying down inside;
If your mother mends a coat cut about and tore;
If the lining's wet and warm – don't you ask no more!

If you meet King George's men, dressed in blue and red,
You be careful what you say, and mindful what is said.
If they call you 'pretty maid', and chuck you 'neath the chin,
Don't you tell where no one is, nor yet where no one's been!

Knocks and footsteps round the house – whistles after dark –
You've no call for running out till the house-dogs bark.
Trusty's here, and *Pincher's* here, and see how dumb they lie –
They don't fret to follow when the Gentlemen go by!

If you do as you've been told, 'likely there's a chance,
You'll be give a dainty doll, all the way from France,
With a cap of Valenciennes, and a velvet hood –
A present from the Gentlemen, along o' being good!
    Five and twenty ponies,
    Trotting through the dark –
    Brandy for the Parson,
    'Baccy for the Clerk;
Them that asks no questions isn't told a lie –
Watch the wall, my darling, while the Gentlemen go by!

Waltzing Matilda

BANJO PATERSON
1864–1941

'Waltzing' is Australian slang for travelling by foot while carrying your possessions in a 'Matilda', which is a type of bag. A 'jumbuck' is a sheep, while a 'coolibah' tree is a kind of eucalyptus that grows beside a 'billabong', or still water found near a river. These words would have been well known to Paterson's fellow Australians when he wrote this poem in 1895.

Oh! there once was a swagman camped in a Billabong
    Under the shade of a Coolibah tree;
And he sang as he looked at his old billy boiling
    'Who'll come a-waltzing Matilda with me?'

Who'll come a-waltzing Matilda, my darling,
    Who'll come a-waltzing Matilda with me?
Waltzing Matilda and leading a water-bag –
    Who'll come a-waltzing Matilda with me?

Down came the jumbuck to drink at the waterhole,
    Up jumped the swagman and grabbed him in glee;
And he sang as he stowed him away in his tucker-bag,
    'You'll come a-waltzing Matilda with me.'

Who'll come a-waltzing Matilda, my darling,
    Who'll come a-waltzing Matilda with me?
Waltzing Matilda and leading a water-bag –
    Who'll come a-waltzing Matilda with me?

Down came the Squatter a-riding his thoroughbred;
    Down came Policeman – one, two, and three.
'Whose is the jumbuck you've got in the tucker-bag?
    You'll come a-waltzing Matilda with me.'

Who'll come a-waltzing Matilda, my darling,
    Who'll come a-waltzing Matilda with me?
Waltzing Matilda and leading a water-bag –
    Who'll come a-waltzing Matilda with me?

But the swagman he up and jumped in the waterhole,
    Drowning himself by the Coolabah tree;
And his ghost may be heard as it sings in the Billabong,
    'Who'll come a-waltzing Matilda with me.'

Who'll come a-waltzing Matilda, my darling,
    Who'll come a-waltzing Matilda with me?
Waltzing Matilda and leading a water-bag –
    Who'll come a-waltzing Matilda with me?

The Wraggle Taggle Gypsies

ANON

This poem most likely dates from the eighteenth century and comes from the Scottish Borders. It is known by other names, such as 'Black Jack Davey', 'The Gypsy Rover' and 'The Three Gypsies'. Many musicians, including Bob Dylan, have used the words of this poem as lyrics.

There were three gypsies a come to my door,
    And downstairs ran this lady, O!
One sang high and another sang low,
    And the other sang bonny, bonny Biscay, O!

Then she pulled off her silk finished gown
    And put on hose of leather, O!
The ragged, ragged rags about our door,
    She's gone with the wraggle taggle gypsies, O!

It was late last night when my lord came home,
    Enquiring for his a-lady, O!
The servants said, on every hand,
    She's gone with the wraggle taggle gypsies, O!

O saddle to me my milk-white steed,
    Go and fetch me my pony, O!
That I may ride and seek my bride,
    Who is gone with the wraggle taggle gypsies, O!

O he rode high and he rode low,
    He rode through woods and copses too,
Until he came to an open field,
    And there he espied his a-lady, O!

What makes you leave your house and land?
  What makes you leave your money, O?
What makes you leave your new wedded lord?
  To go with the wraggle taggle gypsies, O!

What care I for my house and my land?
  What care I for my money, O?
What care I for my new wedded lord?
  I'm off with the wraggle taggle gypsies, O!

Last night you slept on a goose-feather bed,
  With the sheet turned down so bravely, O!
And tonight you'll sleep in a cold open field,
  Along with the wraggle taggle gypsies, O!

What care I for a goose-feather bed?
  With the sheet turned down so bravely, O!
For tonight I shall sleep in a cold open field,
  Along with the wraggle taggle gypsies, O!

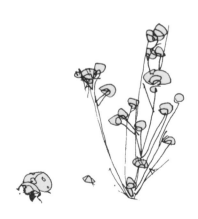

A Visit from St Nicholas

CLEMENT CLARKE MOORE
1779–1863

This poem, also known as 'Twas the Night Before Christmas', was written by Clement Clarke Moore, an American professor of Greek literature, to entertain his children during the Christmas of 1822. A friend later published it without his knowledge, and only when other writers tried to claim it as their own did Clement Clarke Moore reveal that he was the author. This poem helped shape our modern image of Father Christmas delivering presents on Christmas Eve on the back of a sleigh driven by reindeer.

’Twas the night before Christmas, when all through the house
Not a creature was stirring, not even a mouse;
The stockings were hung by the chimney with care,
In hopes that Saint Nicholas soon would be there.
The children were nestled all snug in their beds,
While visions of sugar-plums danced in their heads;
And mamma in her ’kerchief, and I in my cap,
Had just settled down for a long winter’s nap;
When out on the lawn there arose such a clatter,
I sprang from the bed to see what was the matter.
Away to the window I flew like a flash,
Tore open the shutters and threw up the sash.
The moon, on the breast of the new-fallen snow,
Gave the lustre of midday to objects below,

When, what to my wondering eyes should appear,
But a miniature sleigh, and eight tiny reindeer,
With a little old driver, so lively and quick,
I knew in a moment it must be Saint Nick.
More rapid than eagles his coursers they came,
And he whistled, and shouted, and called them by name:
‘Now, *Dasher!* now, *Dancer!* now, *Prancer* and *Vixen!*
On, *Comet!* on, *Cupid!* on, *Donder* and *Blitzen!*
To the top of the porch! to the top of the wall!

Now dash away! dash away! dash away all!'
As dry leaves that before the wild hurricane fly,
When they meet with an obstacle, mount to the sky;
So up to the house-top the coursers they flew,
With the sleigh full of toys, and Saint Nicholas too.
And then, in a twinkling, I heard on the roof
The prancing and pawing of each little hoof –
As I drew in my head, and was turning around,
Down the chimney Saint Nicholas came with a bound.
He was dressed all in fur, from his head to his foot,
And his clothes were all tarnished with ashes and soot;
A bundle of toys he had flung on his back,
And he looked like a peddler just opening his pack.
His eyes – how they twinkled! his dimples, how merry!
His cheeks were like roses, his nose like a cherry!
His droll little mouth was drawn up like a bow,
And the beard of his chin was as white as the snow;
The stump of a pipe he held tight in his teeth,
And the smoke it encircled his head like a wreath;
He had a broad face and a little round belly,
That shook, when he laughed, like a bowlful of jelly.
He was chubby and plump, a right jolly old elf,
And I laughed when I saw him, in spite of myself.
A wink of his eye and a twist of his head,
Soon gave me to know I had nothing to dread.
He spoke not a word, but went straight to his work,
And filled all the stockings; then turned with a jerk,
And laying his finger aside of his nose,
And giving a nod, up the chimney he rose.
He sprang to his sleigh, to his team gave a whistle,
And away they all flew like the down of a thistle.
But I heard him exclaim, ere he drove out of sight,
'Happy Christmas to all, and to all a good-night!'

Sweet Polly Oliver

ANON

As sweet Polly Oliver lay musing in bed,
A sudden strange fancy came into her head.
'Nor father nor mother shall make me false prove,
 I'll 'list as a soldier, and follow my love.'

So early next morning she softly arose,
And dressed herself up in her dead brother's clothes.
She cut her hair close, and she stained her face brown,
And went for a soldier to fair London Town.

Then up spoke the sergeant one day at his drill,
'Now who's good for nursing? A captain, he's ill.'
'I'm ready,' said Polly. To nurse him she's gone,
And finds it's her true love all wasted and wan.

The first week the doctor kept shaking his head,
'No nursing, young fellow, can save him,' he said.
But when Polly Oliver had nursed him back to life
He cried, 'You have cherished him as if you were his wife.'

O then Polly Oliver, she burst into tears
And told the good doctor her hopes and her fears,
And very shortly after, for better or for worse,
The captain took joyfully his pretty soldier nurse.

The Highwayman

ALFRED NOYES
1880–1958

his dramatic tale of a highwayman's pursuit of his lover Bess, and the terrible fate that awaits them, uses many different poetic techniques to engage us in their story – in particular, repetition and alliteration. In the first verse, for example, the word 'riding' is repeated, which brings to life the rhythmic, galloping sound of the actual horse. Alliteration is used throughout the poem. Look, for example, at the first line of the third verse: 'Over the cobbles he clattered and clashed …' The alliteration here adds to the musicality of the poem and also helps you remember the line. See how many examples of alliteration and repetition you can find.

Part One

The wind was a torrent of darkness among the gusty trees.
The moon was a ghostly galleon tossed upon cloudy seas.
The road was a ribbon of moonlight over the purple moor,
And the highwayman came riding –
    Riding – riding –
The highwayman came riding, up to the old inn-door.

He'd a French cocked-hat on his forehead, a bunch of lace at his chin,
A coat of the claret velvet, and breeches of brown doe-skin.
They fitted with never a wrinkle. His boots were up to the thigh.
And he rode with a jewelled twinkle,
    His pistol butts a-twinkle,
His rapier hilt a-twinkle, under the jewelled sky.

Over the cobbles he clattered and clashed in the dark inn-yard.
He tapped with his whip on the shutters, but all was locked and barred.
He whistled a tune to the window, and who should be waiting there

But the landlord's black-eyed daughter,
    Bess, the landlord's daughter,
Plaiting a dark red love-knot into her long black hair.

And dark in the dark old inn-yard a stable-wicket creaked
Where Tim the ostler listened. His face was white and peaked.
His eyes were hollows of madness, his hair like mouldy hay,
But he loved the landlord's daughter,
    The landlord's red-lipped daughter.
Dumb as a dog he listened, and he heard the robber say –

'One kiss, my bonny sweetheart, I'm after a prize tonight,
But I shall be back with the yellow gold before the morning light;
Yet, if they press me sharply, and harry me through the day,
Then look for me by moonlight,
    Watch for me by moonlight,
I'll come to thee by moonlight, though hell should bar the way.'

He rose upright in the stirrups. He scarce could reach her hand,
But she loosened her hair in the casement. His face burnt like a brand
As the black cascade of perfume came tumbling over his breast;
And he kissed its waves in the moonlight,
    (O, sweet black waves in the moonlight!)
Then he tugged at his rein in the moonlight, and galloped away to the west.

Part Two

He did not come in the dawning. He did not come at noon;
And out of the tawny sunset, before the rise of the moon,
When the road was a gypsy's ribbon, looping the purple moor,
A red-coat troop came marching –
    Marching – marching –
King George's men came marching, up to the old inn-door.

They said no word to the landlord. They drank his ale instead.
But they gagged his daughter, and bound her, to the foot of her narrow bed.
Two of them knelt at her casement, with muskets at their side!

There was death at every window;
    And hell at one dark window;
For Bess could see, through her casement, the road that he would ride.

They had tied her up to attention, with many a sniggering jest.
They had bound a musket beside her, with the muzzle beneath her breast!
'Now, keep good watch!' and they kissed her. She heard the doomed man say –
Look for me by moonlight;
    Watch for me by moonlight;
I'll come to thee by moonlight, though hell should bar the way!

She twisted her hands behind her; but all the knots held good!
She writhed her hands till her fingers were wet with sweat or blood!
They stretched and strained in the darkness, and the hours crawled by
  like years,
Till, now, on the stroke of midnight,
    Cold, on the stroke of midnight,
The tip of one finger touched it! The trigger at least was hers!

The tip of one finger touched it. She strove no more for the rest.
Up, she stood up to attention, with the muzzle beneath her breast.
She would not risk their hearing; she would not strive again;
For the road lay bare in the moonlight;
    Blank and bare in the moonlight;
And the blood of her veins, in the moonlight, throbbed to her love's refrain.

Tlot-tlot; tlot-tlot! Had they heard it? The horsehoofs ringing clear;
Tlot-tlot; tlot-tlot, in the distance? Were they deaf that they did not hear?
Down the ribbon of moonlight, over the brow of the hill,
The highwayman came riding –
    Riding – riding –
The red coats looked to their priming! She stood up, straight and still.

Tlot-tlot, in the frosty silence! *Tlot-tlot*, in the echoing night!
Nearer he came and nearer. Her face was like a light.
Her eyes grew wide for a moment; she drew one last deep breath,
Then her finger moved in the moonlight,

Her musket shattered the moonlight,
Shattered her breast in the moonlight and warned him – with her death.

He turned. He spurred to the west; he did not know who stood
Bowed, with her head o'er the musket, drenched with her own red blood!
Not till the dawn he heard it, and his face grew grey to hear
How Bess, the landlord's daughter,
    The landlord's black-eyed daughter,
Had watched for her love in the moonlight, and died in the darkness there.

Back, he spurred like a madman, shouting a curse to the sky,
With the white road smoking behind him and his rapier brandished high.
Blood red were his spurs in the golden noon; wine-red was his velvet coat;
When they shot him down on the highway,
    Down like a dog on the highway,
And he lay in his blood on the highway, with a bunch of lace at his throat.

And still of a winter's night, they say, when the wind is in the trees,
When the moon is a ghostly galleon tossed upon cloudy seas,
When the road is a ribbon of moonlight over the purple moor,
A highwayman comes riding –
    Riding – riding –
A highwayman comes riding, up to the old inn-door.

Over the cobbles he clatters and clangs in the dark inn-yard.
He taps with his whip on the shutters, but all is locked and barred.
He whistles a tune to the window, and who should be waiting there
But the landlord's black-eyed daughter,
    Bess, the landlord's daughter,
Plaiting a dark red love-knot into her long black hair.

Hunter Trials

JOHN BETJEMAN
1906–84

It's awf'lly bad luck on Diana,
  Her ponies have swallowed their bits;
She fished down their throats with a spanner
  And frightened them all into fits.

So now she's attempting to borrow.
  Do lend her some bits, Mummy, *do*;
I'll lend her my own for tomorrow,
  But today *I'll* be wanting them too.

Just look at Prunella on Guzzle,
  The wizardest pony on earth;
Why doesn't she slacken his muzzle
  And tighten the breech in his girth?

I say, Mummy, there's Mrs Geyser
  And doesn't she look pretty sick?
I bet it's because Mona Lisa
  Was hit on the hock with a brick.

Miss Blewitt says Monica threw it,
  But Monica says it was Joan,
And Joan's very thick with Miss Blewitt,
  So Monica's sulking alone.

And Margaret failed in her paces,
  Her withers got tied in a noose,
So her coronets caught in the traces
  And now all her fetlocks are loose.

Oh, it's me now. I'm terribly nervous.
   I wonder if Smudges will shy.
She's practically certain to swerve as
   Her Pelham is over one eye.

Oh wasn't it naughty of Smudges?
   Oh, Mummy, I'm sick with disgust.
She threw me in front of the Judges,
   And my silly old collarbone's bust.

The Inchcape Rock

ROBERT SOUTHEY
1774–1843

Inchcape is a dangerous rock that lurks off the coast of Angus in Scotland. Southey's poem recounts the story of an attempt by a fourteenth-century abbot from Arbroath to place a warning bell on the rock. The bell would allow sailors to be warned of coming danger in the often dark and wild seas in the area. Ralph the Rover, attempting to thwart the kind abbot, is drowned because the bell was not there to save him. There is now a lighthouse on Inchcape Rock designed by Robert Stevenson, the grandfather of the writer Robert Louis Stevenson. It was first used in 1811 and has been praised as one of Britain's most impressive feats of engineering.

No stir in the air, no stir in the sea,
The ship was still as she could be,
Her sails from heaven received no motion,
Her keel was steady in the ocean.

Without either sign or sound of their shock
The waves flowed over the Inchcape Rock;
So little they rose, so little they fell,
They did not move the Inchcape Bell.

The worthy Abbot of Aberbrothok
Had placed that bell on the Inchcape Rock;
On a buoy in the storm it floated and swung,
And over the waves its warning rung.

When the Rock was hid by the surge's swell,
The mariners heard the warning bell;
And then they knew the perilous Rock,
And blest the Abbot of Aberbrothok

The Sun in heaven was shining gay,
All things were joyful on that day;
The sea-birds screamed as they wheeled round,
And there was joyaunce in their sound.

The buoy of the Inchcape Bell was seen
A darker speck on the ocean green;
Sir Ralph the Rover walked his deck,
And fixed his eye on the darker speck.

He felt the cheering power of spring,
It made him whistle, it made him sing;
His heart was mirthful to excess,
But the Rover's mirth was wickedness.

His eye was on the Inchcape float;
Quoth he, 'My men, put out the boat,
And row me to the Inchcape Rock,
And I'll plague the Abbot of Aberbrothok.'

The boat is lowered, the boatmen row,
And to the Inchcape Rock they go;
Sir Ralph bent over from the boat,
And he cut the Bell from the Inchcape float.

Down sank the Bell with a gurgling sound,
The bubbles rose and burst around;
Quoth Sir Ralph, 'The next who comes to the Rock,
Won't bless the Abbot of Aberbrothok.'

Sir Ralph the Rover sailed away,
He scoured the seas for many a day;
And now grown rich with plundered store,
He steers his course for Scotland's shore.

So thick a haze o'er spreads the sky,
They cannot see the Sun on high;
The wind hath blown a gale all day,
At evening it hath died away.

On the deck the Rover takes his stand,
So dark it is they see no land.
Quoth Sir Ralph, 'It will be lighter soon,
For there is the dawn of the rising Moon.'

'Canst hear,' said one, 'the breakers roar?
For methinks we should be near the shore.'
'Now, where we are I cannot tell,
But I wish we could hear the Inchcape Bell.'

They hear no sound, the swell is strong;
Though the wind hath fallen they drift along;
Till the vessel strikes with a shivering shock,
'Oh Christ! It is the Inchcape Rock!'

Sir Ralph the Rover tore his hair!
He curst himself in his despair;
The waves rush in on every side,
The ship is sinking beneath the tide.

But even in his dying fear,
One dreadful sound could the Rover hear;
A sound as if with the Inchcape Bell,
The Devil below was ringing his knell.

The Three Fishers

CHARLES KINGSLEY
1819–75

Three fishers went sailing away to the West,
Away to the West as the sun went down;
Each thought on the woman who loved him the best,
And the children stood watching them out of the town;
For men must work, and women must weep,
And there's little to earn, and many to keep,
Though the harbour bar be moaning.

Three wives sat up in the lighthouse tower,
And they trimmed the lamps as the sun went down;
They looked at the squall, and they looked at the shower,
And the night-rack came rolling up ragged and brown.
But men must work, and women must weep,
Though storms be sudden, and waters deep,
And the harbour bar be moaning.

Three corpses lay out on the shining sands
In the morning gleam as the tide went down,
And the women are weeping and wringing their hands
For those who will never come home to the town;
For men must work, and women must weep,
And the sooner it's over, the sooner to sleep;
And good-bye to the bar and its moaning.

Kubla Khan

SAMUEL TAYLOR COLERIDGE
1772–1834

Samuel Taylor Coleridge was reluctant to publish this poem, saying it had come to him in an opium-induced dream: he described himself sitting in a remote cottage on Exmoor writing the poem in a trance before being interrupted by a visitor.

In Xanadu did Kubla Khan
A stately pleasure-dome decree:
Where Alph, the sacred river, ran
Through caverns measureless to man
 Down to a sunless sea.
So twice five miles of fertile ground
With walls and towers were girdled round:
And there were gardens bright with sinuous rills,
Where blossomed many an incense-bearing tree;
And here were forests ancient as the hills,
Enfolding sunny spots of greenery.

But oh! that deep romantic chasm which slanted
Down the green hill athwart a cedarn cover!
A savage place! as holy and enchanted
As e'er beneath a waning moon was haunted
By woman wailing for her demon-lover!
 And from this chasm, with ceaseless turmoil seething,
As if this earth in fast thick pants were breathing,
A mighty fountain momently was forced:
Amid whose swift half-intermitted burst
Huge fragments vaulted like rebounding hail,
Or chaffy grain beneath the thresher's flail:
And 'mid these dancing rocks at once and ever
It flung up momently the sacred river.

Five miles meandering with a mazy motion
Through wood and dale the sacred river ran,
Then reached the caverns measureless to man,
And sank in tumult to a lifeless ocean:
And 'mid this tumult Kubla heard from far
Ancestral voices prophesying war!
    The shadow of the dome of pleasure
    Floated midway on the waves;
    Where was heard the mingled measure
    From the fountain and the caves.
It was a miracle of rare device,
A sunny pleasure-dome with caves of ice!

    A damsel with a dulcimer
    In a vision once I saw:
    It was an Abyssinian maid,
    And on her dulcimer she played,
    Singing of Mount Abora.
    Could I revive within me
    Her symphony and song,
    To such a deep delight 'twould win me,
That with music loud and long,
I would build that dome in air,
That sunny dome! those caves of ice!
And all who heard should see them there,
And all should cry, Beware! Beware!
His flashing eyes, his floating hair!
Weave a circle round him thrice,
And close your eyes with holy dread,
For he on honey-dew hath fed,
And drunk the milk of Paradise.

Annabel Lee

EDGAR ALLEN POE
1809–49

Edgar Allen Poe considered the death of a beautiful woman the 'most poetical' of subjects, and this poem is a fine example of an elegy, a lament for someone who has died. Critics have disagreed over the identity of Annabel Lee, but it is most likely she is a figment of Poe's melancholic imagination. The plaintive repetition of her name emphasizes the intensity of the narrator's grief and is quite deliberate.

It was many and many a year ago,
    In a kingdom by the sea,
That a maiden there lived whom you may know
    By the name of Annabel Lee;
And this maiden she lived with no other thought
    Than to love and be loved by me.

I was a child and *she* was a child,
    In this kingdom by the sea:
But we loved with a love that was more than love –
    I and my Annabel Lee;
With a love that the winged seraphs of heaven
    Coveted her and me.

And this was the reason that, long ago,
    In this kingdom by the sea,
A wind blew out of a cloud, chilling
    My beautiful Annabel Lee;
So that her highborn kinsman came
    And bore her away from me,
To shut her up in a sepulchre
    In this kingdom by the sea.

The angels, not half so happy in heaven,
    Went envying her and me –
Yes! – that was the reason (as all men know,
    In this kingdom by the sea)
That the wind came out of the cloud by night,
    Chilling and killing my Annabel Lee.

But our love it was stronger by far than the love
    Of those who were older than we –
    Of many far wiser than we –
And neither the angels in Heaven above,
    Nor the demons down under the sea,
Can ever dissever my soul from the soul
    Of the beautiful Annabel Lee.

For the moon never beams, without bringing me dreams
    Of the beautiful Annabel Lee;
And the stars never rise, but I feel the bright eyes
    Of the beautiful Annabel Lee;
And so, all the night-tide, I lie down by the side
    Of my darling – my darling – my life and my bride,
In the sepulchre there by the sea,
    In her tomb by the side of the sea.

Lochinvar

SIR WALTER SCOTT
1771–1832

Written in the form of a traditional ballad, 'Lochinvar' is taken from a much longer narrative poem called 'Marmion'. 'Lochinvar' has eight six-line verses, with three couplets per verse. Lochinvar himself has all the virtues of the archetypal hero: fierce in war, faithful in love and victorious in any undertaking. Note how active and dynamic Lochinvar is compared to the passive qualities of the other characters in this poem. When 'Marmion' was first published, the critics disliked it, but this did nothing to diminish its popularity among the public, who bought copies by the thousand.

O, young Lochinvar is come out of the west,
Through all the wide Border his steed was the best;
And save his good broadsword he weapons had none,
He rode all unarm'd, and he rode all alone.
So faithful in love, and so dauntless in war,
There never was knight like the young Lochinvar.

He staid not for brake, and he stopp'd not for stone,
He swam the Eske river where ford there was none;
But ere he alighted at Netherby gate,
The bride had consented, the gallant came late:
For a laggard in love, and a dastard in war,
Was to wed the fair Ellen of brave Lochinvar.

So boldly he enter'd the Netherby Hall,
Among bride's-men, and kinsmen, and brothers and all:
Then spoke the bride's father, his hand on his sword,
(For the poor craven bridegroom said never a word,)
'O come ye in peace here, or come ye in war,
Or to dance at our bridal, young Lord Lochinvar?'

'I long woo'd your daughter, my suit you denied;
Love swells like the Solway, but ebbs like its tide –
And now I am come, with this lost love of mine,
To lead but one measure, drink one cup of wine.
There are maidens in Scotland more lovely by far,
That would gladly be bride to the young Lochinvar.'

The bride kiss'd the goblet: the knight took it up,
He quaff'd off the wine, and he threw down the cup.
She look'd down to blush, and she look'd up to sigh,
With a smile on her lips, and a tear in her eye.
He took her soft hand, ere her mother could bar,
'Now tread we a measure!' said young Lochinvar.

So stately his form, and so lovely her face,
That never a hall such a galliard did grace;
While her mother did fret, and her father did fume,
And the bridegroom stood dangling his bonnet and plume;
And the bride-maidens whisper'd, ''Twere better by far
To have match'd our fair cousin with young Lochinvar.'

One touch to her hand, and one word in her ear,
When they reach'd the hall-door, and the charger stood near;
So light to the croupe the fair lady he swung,
So light to the saddle before her he sprung!
'She is won! we are gone, over bank, bush, and scaur;
They'll have fleet steeds that follow,' quoth young Lochinvar.

There was mounting 'mong Graemes of the Netherby clan;
Forsters, Fenwicks, and Musgraves, they rode and they ran:
There was racing and chasing on Cannobie Lee,
But the lost bride of Netherby ne'er did they see.
So daring in love, and so dauntless in war,
Have ye e'er heard of gallant like young Lochinvar?

The Lady of Shalott

ALFRED, LORD TENNYSON
1809–92

'The Lady of Shalott' is a ballad inspired by the legendary tales of King Arthur and his Knights of the Round Table. Sir Lancelot is the bravest and most famous of Arthur's knights. With its pastoral setting and vivid scenes of medieval life, the story of the Lady of Shalott and her doomed love for Sir Lancelot is one of our favourite poems. Here's a challenge: can you learn the whole thing by heart, as we were asked to when we were at school?

Part I

On either side the river lie
Long fields of barley and of rye,
That clothe the wold and meet the sky;
And thro' the field the road runs by
    To many-tower'd Camelot;
And up and down the people go,
Gazing where the lilies blow
Round an island there below,
    The island of Shalott.

Willows whiten, aspens quiver,
Little breezes dusk and shiver
Thro' the wave that runs for ever
By the island in the river
    Flowing down to Camelot.
Four gray walls, and four gray towers,
Overlook a space of flowers,
And the silent isle imbowers
    The Lady of Shalott.

By the margin, willow-veil'd
Slide the heavy barges trail'd
By slow horses; and unhail'd
The shallop flitteth silken-sail'd
    Skimming down to Camelot:
But who hath seen her wave her hand?
Or at the casement seen her stand?
Or is she known in all the land,
    The Lady of Shalott?

Only reapers, reaping early
In among the bearded barley,
Hear a song that echoes cheerly
From the river winding clearly,
    Down to tower'd Camelot:
And by the moon the reaper weary,
Piling sheaves in uplands airy,
Listening, whispers ''Tis the fairy
    Lady of Shalott.'

Part II

There she weaves by night and day
A magic web with colours gay.
She has heard a whisper say,
A curse is on her if she stay
    To look down to Camelot.
She knows not what the curse may be,
And so she weaveth steadily,
And little other care hath she,
    The Lady of Shalott.

And moving thro' a mirror clear
That hangs before her all the year,
Shadows of the world appear.
There she sees the highway near
    Winding down to Camelot:
There the river eddy whirls,
And there the surly village-churls,
And the red cloaks of market girls,
    Pass onward from Shalott.

Sometimes a troop of damsels glad,
An abbot on an ambling pad,
Sometimes a curly shepherd-lad,
Or long-hair'd page in crimson clad,
    Goes by to tower'd Camelot;
And sometimes thro' the mirror blue
The knights come riding two and two:
She hath no loyal knight and true,
    The Lady of Shalott.

But in her web she still delights
To weave the mirror's magic sights,
For often thro' the silent nights
A funeral, with plumes and lights,
    And music, went to Camelot:
Or when the moon was overhead,
Came two young lovers lately wed;
'I am half-sick of shadows,' said
    The Lady of Shalott.

Part III

A bow-shot from her bower-eaves,
He rode between the barley sheaves,
The sun came dazzling thro' the leaves,
And flamed upon the brazen greaves
    Of bold Sir Lancelot.
A red-cross knight for ever kneel'd
To a lady in his shield,
That sparkled on the yellow field,
    Beside remote Shalott.

The gemmy bridle glitter'd free,
Like to some branch of stars we see
Hung in the golden Galaxy.
The bridle bells rang merrily
    As he rode down to Camelot:
And from his blazon'd baldric slung
A mighty silver bugle hung,

And as he rode his armour rung,
    Beside remote Shalott.

All in the blue unclouded weather
Thick-jewell'd shone the saddle-leather,
The helmet and the helmet-feather
Burn'd like one burning flame together,
    As he rode down to Camelot.
As often thro' the purple night,
Below the starry clusters bright,
Some bearded meteor, trailing light,
    Moves over still Shalott.

His broad clear brow in sunlight glow'd;
On burnish'd hooves his war-horse trode;
From underneath his helmet flow'd
His coal-black curls as on he rode,
    As he rode down to Camelot.
From the bank and from the river
He flash'd into the crystal mirror,
'Tirra lirra,' by the river
    Sang Sir Lancelot.

She left the web, she left the loom,
She made three paces thro' the room,
She saw the water-lily bloom,
She saw the helmet and the plume,
    She look'd down to Camelot.
Out flew the web and floated wide;
The mirror crack'd from side to side;
'The curse is come upon me,' cried
    The Lady of Shalott.

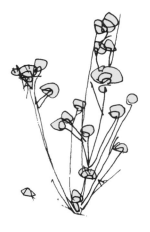

Part IV

In the stormy east-wind straining,
The pale yellow woods were waning,
The broad stream in his banks complaining,
Heavily the low sky raining
   Over tower'd Camelot;
Down she came and found a boat
Beneath a willow left afloat,
And round about the prow she wrote
   The Lady of Shalott.

And down the river's dim expanse
Like some bold seer in a trance,
Seeing all his own mischance –
With a glassy countenance
   Did she look to Camelot.
And at the closing of the day
She loosed the chain, and down she lay;
The broad stream bore her far away,
   The Lady of Shalott.

Lying, robed in snowy white
That loosely flew to left and right –
The leaves upon her falling light –
Thro' the noises of the night
   She floated down to Camelot:
And as the boat-head wound along
The willowy hills and fields among,
They heard her singing her last song,
   The Lady of Shalott.

Heard a carol, mournful, holy,
Chanted loudly, chanted lowly,
Till her blood was frozen slowly,
And her eyes were darken'd wholly,
    Turn'd to tower'd Camelot;
For ere she reach'd upon the tide
The first house by the water-side,
Singing in her song she died,
    The Lady of Shalott.

Under tower and balcony,
By garden-wall and gallery,
A gleaming shape she floated by,
Dead-pale between the houses high,
    Silent into Camelot.
Out upon the wharfs they came,
Knight and burgher, lord and dame,
And round the prow they read her name,
    The Lady of Shalott.

Who is this? and what is here?
And in the lighted palace near
Died the sound of royal cheer;
And they cross'd themselves for fear,
    All the knights at Camelot:
But Lancelot mused a little space;
He said, 'She has a lovely face;
God in his mercy lend her grace,
    The Lady of Shalott.'

The Hat

CAROL ANN DUFFY
1955–

Duffy composed this poem using some of the most famous lines in English-language poetry, written by some of our most famous poets. We love this unusual, non-rhyming poem and how the hat journeys through time, passing from the old poets to the new. The way the lines cleverly run on from one to the next is called enjambment, which we explain on page 268.

I was on Chaucer's head when he said He was a verray,
parfit gentil knyght, and tossed me into the air. I landed
on Thomas Wyatt's hair as he thought They fle from me
that sometyme did me seek, then left me behind in an Inn.
Sir Philip Sidney strolled in, picked me up, saying
My true love hath my hart and I have his, then hoopla'd me
straight onto William Shakespeare's head as he said
Tell me where is fancie bred, and passed me along
to John Donne, who was wearing me as he sang Go
and catch a falling star, but handed me on to one leaving
the bar, name of Herbert, George, who wore me up top
like a halo, murmured Love bade me welcome, yet my soul
drew back, then lay me dreamily down at the end of a pew
in a church. I was there for a while, dwelling on heaven
and hell, till Andrew Marvell arrived, said Had we
but World enough and Time, and filled me up to the brim
with blooms to give to a girl. She kept the flowers,
but handed me on to warm the crown of a balding chap,
named Milton, John, who sported me the day he happened
to say They also serve who only stand and wait,
then threw me over a gate. I fell in the path of Robert Herrick,
who scooped me up with a shout of Gather ye rosebuds
while ye may! and later gave me away to Dryden, John,
who tried me on for size, saying None but the brave
deserves the fair, then let me drop. I was soon picked up
by a bloke, Alexander Pope, who admitted the gen'ral rule

that every poet's a fool with cheerful grace, then tilted me
over the face of Christopher Smart, who loved his cat, said
For first he looks upon his forepaws to see if they
are clean, and let the kitty kip in myself, The Hat. I was saved
from that by William Blake, who liked the extra inch or two
I gave to his height as he bawled out Tyger, Tyger, burning
bright in the forests of the night, then bartered me
for the price of a mutton pie to Robbie Burns, who stared
in the mirror, grunted O, wad some Pow'r the giftie gie us
to see oursels as others see us! and threw me out
of the window. S. T. Coleridge passed, muttering Water,
water, everywhere, nor any drop to drink, and bore me
off to the Lakes to give as a gift to Wordsworth. Will
wore me to keep out the cold on a stroll when, all at once,
he said that he saw a crowd, a host of golden daffodils,
and lobbed me high with delight! It was late at night
when Byron came, mad, bad, bit of a lad, insisting So,
we'll go no more a roving, as he kicked me into a tree.
A breeze blew me gently down from my branch to flop
onto Shelley's head as he said O, Wind, if Winter comes,
can Spring be far behind? But Keats sneaked up,
snatched me away wore me the night he claimed
I cannot see what flowers are at my feet, and left me
snagged on a bush in the gathering dark of a park.
John Clare came along, shouted I am, yet what I am
none cares or knows, and jammed me down
on his puzzled brow as he made for the open road.
Then Tennyson, Alfred, Lord, thundered past on a horse
and yanked me off, yelled Into the Valley of Death
rode the six hundred! I flew from his head as he galloped
away, and settled on Browning's crown as he said This
to you – my moon of poets, and got down on one knee
to present Little Me to Elizabeth Barrett. I liked it up there
snug on her shiny hair, as she cooed How do I love thee,
let me count the ways, but she handed me down
for Emily Brontë to wear on the moors as she wailed
Fifteen wild Decembers from those brown hills have melted
into Spring, then a blast of wind blew me to the edge of the sea
where Matthew Arnold wore me to keep off the spray

when he said Listen! You hear the grating roar of pebbles
which the waves draw back, and lobbed me over the foam
like a boy with a stone. I bobbed away like a boat,
till fished from the drink on t'other side of the pond
by Whitman Walt who wrung me dry and flung me high
as he bawled Behold, I do not give lectures or a little
charity, when I give I give myself, and sent me on with a kiss
to Emily Dickinson She popped me into a hat-box, along
with a note that read This is my letter to the world,
that never wrote to me, then posted me over land and sea
to Christina Rossetti, who used me to keep the blazing sun
from her face as she asked Does the road wind up-hill
all the way? The reply being yes, she considered it best
to hand me to Hopkins, Gerard Manley, whose head
I adorned as he warmly intoned Glory be to God
for dappled things, but I fell to the ground as he stared
at the sky. Thomas Hardy came sauntering by, spied me
and tried me, said I am the family face; flesh perishes,
I live on, and tossed me to one who stood on his own
by a tree – Housman, A. E. He sported me, saying Lads
in their hundreds to Ludlow come in for the fair, but lost me,
while arm-wrestling there in a bar, to Kipling, Rudyard,
who fiddled with me the day he pronounced If you can meet
with triumph and disaster and treat those two impostors
just the same, then carelessly left me behind in the back
of a cab. Next in was an Irish chap, W B. Yeats, who gave
the driver a tip, carried me off to wear at a tilt on his head
as he said Tread softly because you tread on my dreams,
so Charlotte Mew bore me away, murmured no year
has been like this that has just gone by, and started to cry.
A train sighed by. Edward Thomas leaned out, said
Yes, I remember Adlestrop, and lifted me up, but a cold wind
blew me Wilfred Owen's way; he turned me sadly round
and around in his hands and asked What passing-bells
for these who die as cattle? then hurled me back
at the wind. I was seized as I flew by Ezra Pound,
who wore me out and about, saying Winter is
icummen in, Lhude sing Goddamn! then posted me
into the safety deposit box of the bank where T. S. Eliot

worked. April, he said, is the cruellest month, and used me
to keep off the rain, leaving me lying behind on a bench
when the sun came out. I was found by MacDiarmid, Hugh,
and was warming the egg of his head when he said I'll ha'e
nae hauf-way hoose, but aye be whaur extremes meet –
then dropped me down at the feet of Lawrence, D. H.,
who picked me up and was modelling me as he mused
I never saw a wild thing sorry for itself, then chucked me over
to Robert Graves. He pulled me low on his head and said
There's a cool web of language winds us in, then began
to nod off. I was pinched from his brow by Riding, Laura,
who was trying me on as she thought The wind suffers
of blowing, the sea suffers of water, then squashed me
down onto Dylan Thomas's curls. Do not, he said,
go gentle into that good night, then sold me on
for the price of a pint to Louis MacNeice. He wore me
when he said World is crazier and more of it
than we think, then decided to give me to Auden, W. H.
He was delighted, wore me all night, said the desires
of the heart are as crooked as corkscrews, but left me
behind the next day in the loo. John Betjeman found me,
smoothed, dusted-down me, and popped me on
as he trilled Come, friendly bombs, then flopped me on
to the head of Philip Larkin, who cycled past, saying
Man hands on misery to man, then stopped at a church
and handed me on by the graves to Stevie Smith,
who wore me on holiday with her aunt, where she said
I was much further out than you thought, and not waving
but drowning. I was all at sea, till Elizabeth Bishop deftly
hooked me, said I caught a tremendous fish, and held him
beside the boat, then left me behind on an airport seat
for Robert Lowell to find and put on for the flight over
to England. He arrived and declared Everywhere,
giant finned cars nose forward like fish, and gave me
to Sylvia Plath. Dying, she said, is an art like everything else,
and left me to Hughes, Ted, man in black, who growled
with a sudden sharp hot stink of fox it enters the dark hole
of the head . . . but whose head, whose head, whose head,
whose head, whose head, whose will I settle on next?

The Raven

EDGAR ALLEN POE
1809–49

After falling asleep whilst reading a book, the young man who narrates this poem is woken up by a stranger tapping at his door. Already distressed by the loss of his love, he is gradually driven mad by the haunting visitor. With its strange story and echoing rhymes ('more', 'door' and 'nevermore'), this poem might send a tingle up your spine, just like a ghost story. The word 'Plutonian' refers to Pluto, the Roman god of the underworld.

Once upon a midnight dreary, while I pondered, weak and weary,
Over many a quaint and curious volume of forgotten lore –
While I nodded, nearly napping, suddenly there came a tapping,
As of some one gently rapping, rapping at my chamber door.
''Tis some visitor,' I muttered, 'tapping at my chamber door –
   Only this, and nothing more.'

Ah, distinctly I remember it was in the bleak December,
And each separate dying ember wrought its ghost upon the floor.
Eagerly I wished the morrow; – vainly I had sought to borrow
From my books surcease of sorrow – sorrow for the lost Lenore –
For the rare and radiant maiden whom the angels named Lenore –
   Nameless here for evermore.

And the silken sad uncertain rustling of each purple curtain
Thrilled me – filled me with fantastic terrors never felt before;
So that now, to still the beating of my heart, I stood repeating
''Tis some visitor entreating entrance at my chamber door –
Some late visitor entreating entrance at my chamber door; –
   This it is, and nothing more.'

Presently my soul grew stronger; hesitating then no longer,
'Sir,' said I, 'or Madam, truly your forgiveness I implore;
But the fact is I was napping, and so gently you came rapping,
And so faintly you came tapping, tapping at my chamber door,
That I scarce was sure I heard you' – here I opened wide the door; –
 Darkness there, and nothing more.

Deep into that darkness peering, long I stood there wondering, fearing,
Doubting, dreaming dreams no mortal ever dared to dream before;
But the silence was unbroken, and the darkness gave no token,
And the only word there spoken was the whispered word, 'Lenore!'
This I whispered, and an echo murmured back the word, 'Lenore!'
 Merely this and nothing more.

Back into the chamber turning, all my soul within me burning.
Soon again I heard a tapping somewhat louder than before.
'Surely,' said I, 'surely that is something at my window lattice;
Let me see, then, what thereat is, and this mystery explore –
Let my heart be still a moment, and this mystery explore; –
 'Tis the wind and nothing more!'

Open here I flung the shutter, when, with many a flirt and flutter,
In there stepped a stately raven of the saintly days of yore.
Not the least obeisance made he; not an instant stopped or stayed he;
But, with mien of lord or lady, perched above my chamber door –
Perched upon a bust of Pallas just above my chamber door –
 Perched, and sat, and nothing more.

Then this ebony bird beguiling my sad fancy into smiling,
By the grave and stern decorum of the countenance it wore,
'Though thy crest be shorn and shaven, thou,' I said, 'art sure no craven.
Ghastly grim and ancient raven wandering from the Nightly shore –
Tell me what thy lordly name is on the Night's Plutonian shore!'
 Quoth the raven, 'Nevermore.'

Much I marvelled this ungainly fowl to hear discourse so plainly,
Though its answer little meaning – little relevancy bore;
For we cannot help agreeing that no living human being
Ever yet was blessed with seeing bird above his chamber door –
Bird or beast upon the sculptured bust above his chamber door,
   With such name as 'Nevermore'.

But the raven, sitting lonely on the placid bust, spoke only,
That one word, as if his soul in that one word he did outpour.
Nothing further then he uttered – not a feather then he fluttered –
Till I scarcely more than muttered, 'Other friends have flown before –
On the morrow *he* will leave me, as my hopes have flown before.'
   Then the bird said, 'Nevermore.'

Startled at the stillness broken by reply so aptly spoken,
'Doubtless,' said I, 'what it utters is its only stock and store,
Caught from some unhappy master, whom unmerciful Disaster
Followed fast and followed faster till his songs one burden bore –
Till the dirges of his Hope that melancholy burden bore
   Of "Never – nevermore".'

But the raven still beguiling all my sad soul into smiling,
Straight I wheeled a cushioned seat in front of bird and bust and door;
Then, upon the velvet sinking, I betook myself to linking
Fancy unto fancy, thinking what this ominous bird of yore –
What this grim, ungainly, ghastly, gaunt, and ominous bird of yore
   Meant in croaking 'Nevermore.'

This I sat engaged in guessing, but no syllable expressing
To the fowl whose fiery eyes now burned into my bosom's core;
This and more I sat divining, with my head at ease reclining
On the cushion's velvet violet lining that the lamp-light gloated o'er,
But whose velvet violet lining with the lamp-light gloating o'er,
   She shall press, ah, nevermore!

Then, methought, the air grew denser, perfumed from an unseen censer
Swung by Seraphim whose foot-falls tinkled on the tufted floor.
'Wretch,' I cried, 'thy God hath lent thee – by these angels he has sent thee
Respite – respite and nepenthe from thy memories of Lenore!
Quaff, oh quaff this kind nepenthe, and forget this lost Lenore!'
                    Quoth the raven, 'Nevermore.'

'Prophet!' said I, 'thing of evil! – prophet still, if bird or devil! –
Whether Tempter sent, or whether tempest tossed thee here ashore,
Desolate yet all undaunted, on this desert land enchanted –
On this home by Horror haunted – tell me truly, I implore –
Is there – *is* there balm in Gilead? – tell me – tell me, I implore!'
                    Quoth the raven, 'Nevermore.'

'Prophet!' said I, 'thing of evil! – prophet still, if bird or devil!
By that Heaven that bends above us – by that God we both adore –
Tell this soul with sorrow laden if, within the distant Aidenn,
It shall clasp a sainted maiden whom the angels named Lenore –
Clasp a rare and radiant maiden, whom the angels named Lenore?'
                    Quoth the raven, 'Nevermore.'

'Be that word our sign of parting, bird or fiend!' I shrieked, upstarting –
'Get thee back into the tempest and the Night's Plutonian shore!
Leave no black plume as a token of that lie thy soul hath spoken!
Leave my loneliness unbroken! – quit the bust above my door!'
Take thy beak from out my heart, and take thy form from off my door!'
                    Quoth the raven, 'Nevermore.'

And the raven, never flitting, still is sitting, still is sitting
On the pallid bust of Pallas just above my chamber door;
And his eyes have all the seeming of a demon's that is dreaming,
And the lamp-light o'er him streaming throws his shadow on the floor;
And my soul from out that shadow that lies floating on the floor
                    Shall be lifted – nevermore!

Magic

The Little Elf-man

JOHN KENDRICK BANGS
1862–1922

This short ballad uses a strict verse form, which has an 'abcb' rhyme scheme. This rhyme scheme is often used in songs because of its regularity and the way it draws you to the end of the verse when spoken aloud. As well as writing funny stories and poems, Bangs was a journalist in New York at Harper's magazine and held the title 'Editor of the Departments of Humour'.

I met a little elf-man once,
　　Down where the lilies blow.
I asked him why he was so small,
　　And why he didn't grow.

He slightly frowned, and with his eye
　　He looked me through and through –
'I'm quite as big for me,' said he,
　　'As you are big for you!'

Silver

WALTER DE LA MARE
1873–1956

In this poem, Walter de la Mare uses sibilance (alliteration using the letter 's') and personification, whereby the moon becomes a person to convey the magic of moonlight.

Slowly, silently, now the moon
Walks the night in her silver shoon;
This way, and that, she peers, and sees
Silver fruit upon silver trees;
One by one the casements catch
Her beams beneath the silvery thatch;
Couched in his kennel, like a log,
With paws of silver sleeps the dog;
From their shadowy cote the white breasts peep
Of doves in silver-feathered sleep;
A harvest mouse goes scampering by,
With silver claws, and silver eye;
And moveless fish in the water gleam,
By silver reeds in a silver stream.

The Fairies

WILLIAM ALLINGHAM
1824–89

This poem was inspired by Irish folklore. Although the poet initially presents the fairies as faintly comic in their gaily coloured clothes, he goes on to reveal that they are feared by their human neighbours. Like other fairy-tales, this poem blends the picturesque and the sinister to unsettle the reader. The first lines of the poem have been used by other writers and are given to the character of the Tinker in the film Willy Wonka and the Chocolate Factory *when he refers to the Oompa-Loompas.*

Up the airy mountain,
Down the rushy glen,
We daren't go a-hunting,
For fear of little men;
Wee folk, good folk,
Trooping all together;
Green jacket, red cap,
And white owl's feather!

Down along the rocky shore
Some make their home,
They live on crispy pancakes
Of yellow tide-foam;
Some in the reeds
Of the black mountain-lake,
With frogs for their watch-dogs,
All night awake.

High on the hill-top
The old King sits;
He is now so old and grey,
He's nigh lost his wits.
With a bridge of white mist

Columbkill he crosses,
On his stately journeys
From Slieveleague to Rosses;
Or going up with music,
On cold starry nights,
To sup with the Queen
Of the gay Northern Lights.

They stole little Bridget
For seven years long;
When she came down again
Her friends were all gone.
They took her lightly back
Between the night and morrow;
They thought she was fast asleep,
But she was dead with sorrow.
They have kept her ever since
Deep within the lake,
On a bed of flag-leaves,
Watching till she wake.

By the craggy hillside,
Through the mosses bare,
They have planted thorn-trees
For pleasure here and there.
Is any man so daring
As dig them up in spite,
He shall find the thornies set
In his bed at night.

Up the airy mountain,
Down the rushy glen,
We daren't go a-hunting,
For fear of little men;
Wee folk, good folk,
Trooping all together;
Green jacket, red cap,
And white owl's feather!

Over Hill, Over Dale

WILLIAM SHAKESPEARE
1564–1616

This poem comes from Act 2, Scene 1 of Shakespeare's A Midsummer Night's Dream, *and is spoken by a fairy.*

Over hill, over dale,
    Thorough bush, thorough briar,
Over park, over pale,
    Thorough blood, thorough fire,
I do wander everywhere,
Swifter than the moon's sphere;
And I serve the Fairy Queen,
To dew her orbs upon the green.
The cowslips tall her pensioners be:
In their gold coats spots you see;
Those be rubies, fairy favours,
In those freckles live their savours:
I must go seek some dewdrops here,
And hang a pearl in every cowslip's ear.
Farewell, thou lob of spirits; I'll be gone:
Our queen and all her elves come here anon.

Fairy Days

WILLIAM MAKEPEACE THACKERAY
1811–63

'Fairy Days' recalls the simple pleasure of being told stories as a child. Thackeray conjures up images of princesses and knights, queens and fairies, which are reminiscent of old English fairy-tales.

Beside the old hall-fire upon my nurse's knee,
Of happy fairy days what tales were told to me!
I thought the world was once all peopled with princesses,
And my heart would beat to hear their loves and their distresses:
And many a quiet night, in slumber sweet and deep,
The pretty fairy people would visit me in sleep.

I saw them in my dreams come flying east and west,
With wondrous fairy gifts the newborn babe they bless'd;
One has brought a jewel and one a crown of gold,
And one has brought a curse but she is wrinkled and old.
The gentle queen turns pale to hear those words of sin,
But the king he only laughs and bids the dance begin.

The babe has grown to be the fairest of the land,
And rides the forest green, a hawk upon her hand,
An ambling palfrey white, a golden robe and crown:
I've seen her in my dreams riding up and down:
And heard the ogre laugh as she fell into his snare,
At the little tender creature who wept and tore her hair!

But ever when it seemed her need was at the sorest,
A prince in shining mail comes prancing through the forest,
A waving ostrich-plume, a buckler burnished bright;
I've seen him in my dreams good sooth! A gallant knight.
His lips are coral red beneath a dark moustache;
See how he waves his hand and how his blue eyes flash!

'Come forth, thou Paynim knight!' he shouts in accents clear.
The giant and the maid both tremble his voice to hear.
Saint Mary guard him well! he draws his falchion keen,
The giant and the knight are fighting on the green.
I see them in my dreams – his blade gives stroke on stroke,
The giant pants and reels and tumbles like an oak!

With what a blushing grace he falls upon his knee
And takes the lady's hand and whispers, 'You are free!'
Ah! happy childish tales of knight and faerie!
I waken from my dreams but there's ne'er a knight for me;
I waken from my dreams and wish that I could be
A child by the old hall-fire upon my nurse's knee!

Double, Double, Toil and Trouble

WILLIAM SHAKESPEARE
1564–1616

This is a perfect poem to learn by heart: the rhymes and gruesome ingredients make it almost impossible to forget. It is from Act 4, Scene 1 of the play Macbeth, *in which the witches prophesy that Macbeth, a powerful Scottish lord, will become King. The play is known as one of Shakespeare's tragedies, as the main character meets a sticky end due to his own flaws. Although this potion and spell work in the play, it is perhaps unwise to try making it yourself!*

ALL
Double, double, toil and trouble;
Fire burn, and cauldron bubble.

SECOND WITCH
Fillet of a fenny snake,
In the cauldron boil and bake;
Eye of newt and toe of frog,
Wool of bat and tongue of dog,
Adder's fork and blind-worm's sting,
Lizard's leg and owlet's wing,
For a charm of powerful trouble,
Like a hell-broth boil and bubble.

ALL
Double, double, toil and trouble;
Fire burn, and cauldron bubble.

The Forsaken Merman

MATTHEW ARNOLD
1822–88

Come, dear children, let us away;
Down and away below!
Now my brothers call from the bay,
Now the great winds shoreward blow,
Now the salt tides seaward flow;
Now the wild white horses play,
Champ and chafe and toss in the spray.
Children dear, let us away.
This way, this way!

Call her once before you go –
Call once yet!
In a voice that she will know:
'Margaret! Margaret!'
Children's voices should be dear
(Call once more) to a mother's ear;
Children's voices, wild with pain –
Surely she will come again!
Call her once and come away;
This way, this way!
'Mother dear, we cannot stay!
The wild white horses foam and fret.'
Margaret! Margaret!

Come, dear children, come away down;
Call no more!
One last look at the white-wall'd town,
And the little grey church on the windy shore.
Then come down!
She will not come though you call all day;
Come away, come away!
Children dear, was it yesterday

We heard the sweet bells over the bay?
In the caverns where we lay,
Through the surf and through the swell,
The far-off sound of a silver bell?
Sand-strewn caverns, cool and deep,
Where the winds are all asleep;
Where the spent lights quiver and gleam,
Where the salt weed sways in the stream,
Where the sea-beasts, ranged all round,
Feed in the ooze of their pasture-ground;
Where the sea-snakes coil and twine,
Dry their mail and bask in the brine;
Where great whales come sailing by,
Sail and sail, with unshut eye,
Round the world for ever and aye?
When did music come this way?
Children dear, was it yesterday?

Children dear, was it yesterday
(Call yet once) that she went away?
Once she sate with you and me,
On a red gold throne in the heart of the sea,
And the youngest sate on her knee.
She comb'd its bright hair, and she tended it well,
When down swung the sound of the far-off bell.
She sigh'd, she look'd up through the clear green sea;
She said, 'I must go, for my kinsfolk pray
In the little grey church on the shore to-day.
'Twill be Easter-time in the world- ah me!
And I lose my poor soul, Merman, here with thee.'
I said, 'Go up, dear heart, through the waves;
Say thy prayer, and come back to the kind sea-caves!'
She smiled, she went up through the surf in the bay.
Children dear, was it yesterday?

Children dear, were we long alone?
'The sea grows stormy, the little ones moan.
Long prayers,' I said, 'in the world they say;
Come!' I said, and we rose through the surf in the bay.

We went up the beach, by the sandy down
Where the sea-stocks bloom, to the white-wall'd town.
Through the narrow paved streets, where all was still,
To the little grey church on the windy hill.
From the church came a murmur of folk at their prayers,
But we stood without in the cold blowing airs.
We climb'd on the graves, on the stones worn with rains,
And we gazed up the aisle through the small leaded panes.
She sate by the pillar; we saw her clear:
'Margaret, hist! come quick, we are here!
Dear heart,' I said, 'we are long alone;
The sea grows stormy, the little ones moan.'
But, ah! she gave me never a look,
For her eyes were seal'd to the holy book!
Loud prays the priest; shut stands the door
Came away, children, call no more!
Come away, come down, call no more!

Down, down, down!
Down to the depths of the sea!
She sits at her wheel in the humming town,
Singing most joyfully.
Hark what she sings: 'O joy, O joy,
For the humming street, and the child with its toy!
For the priest, and the bell, and the holy well;
For the wheel where I spun,
And the blessed light of the sun!'
And so she sings her fill,
Singing most joyfully,
Till the shuttle falls from her hand,
And the whizzing wheel stands still.
She steals to the window, and looks at the sand,
And over the sand at the sea;
And her eyes are set in a stare;
And anon there breaks a sigh,
And anon there drops a tear,
From a sorrow-clouded eye,
And a heart sorrow-laden,
A long, long sigh;

For the cold strange eyes of a little Mermaiden
And the gleam of her golden hair.

Come away, away, children:
Come children, come down!
The hoarse wind blows colder;
Lights shine in the town.
She will start from her slumber
When gusts shake the door;
She will hear the winds howling,
Will hear the waves roar.
We shall see, while above us
The waves roar and whirl,
A ceiling of amber,
A pavement of pearl.
Singing: 'Here came a mortal,
But faithless was she!
And alone dwell for ever
The kings of the sea.'

But, children, at midnight,
When soft the winds blow,
When clear falls the moonlight,
When spring-tides are low;
When sweet airs come seaward
From heaths starr'd with broom,
And high rocks throw mildly
On the blanch'd sands a gloom;
Up the still, glistening beaches,
Up the creeks we will hie,
Over banks of bright seaweed
The ebb-tide leaves dry.
We will gaze, from the sand-hills,
At the white, sleeping town;
At the church on the hill-side –
And then come back down.
Singing, 'There dwells a loved one,
But cruel is she!
She left lonely for ever
The kings of the sea.'

Sabrina Fair

JOHN MILTON
1608–74

*P*art of a festive court entertainment by John Milton called 'Comus', 'Sabrina
*Fair' is filled with mythological references. Tethys, Nereus, Glaucus and many
of the other names mentioned in the poem were Greek gods and goddesses of the sea.
In the seventeenth century, poetry readers would have been well versed in Latin and
familiar with classical figures. Milton also wrote the epic poem 'Paradise Lost'.*

> *Sabrina fair,*
> *Listen where thou art sitting*
> *Under the glassy, cool, translucent wave,*
> *In twisted braids of lilies knitting*
> *The loose train of thy amber-dropping hair;*
> *Listen for dear honour's sake,*
> *Goddess of the silver lake,*
> *Listen and save.*

Listen and appear to us
In name of great Oceanus,
By the earth-shaking Neptune's mace,
And Tethys' grave majestic pace,
By hoary Nereus, wrinkled look,
And the Carpathian wizard's hook,
By scaly Triton's winding shell,
And old sooth-saying Glaucus' spell,
By Leucothea's lovely hands,
And her son that rules the strands,
By Thetis' tinsel-slipper'd feet,
And the songs of Sirens sweet,
By dead Parthenope's dear tomb,
And fair Ligea's golden comb,
Wherewith she sits on diamond rocks
Sleeking her soft alluring locks,

By all the nymphs that nightly dance
Upon thy streams with wily glance,
Rise, rise, and heave thy rosy head
From thy coral-paven bed,
And bridle in thy headlong wave,
Till thou our summons answered have.
                    Listen and save.

Sabrina rises, attended by water-nymphs, and sings.
   By the rushy-fringèd bank,
Where grows the willow and the osier dank,
   My sliding chariot stays,
Thick set with agate, and the azurn sheen
Of turkis blue and emerald green
   That in the channel strays,
Whilst from off the waters fleet
Thus I set my printless feet
O'er the cowslip's velvet head,
   That bends not as I tread.
Gentle swain, at thy request
   I am here.

The Elf Singing

WILLIAM ALLINGHAM
1824–89

William Allingham uses pairs of rhyming couplets, but then cleverly breaks the rhythm. In this poem the couplets, along with the varied verse lengths, give a feeling of jauntiness. As you read, you can almost feel the Elf dodging to avoid the Wizard creeping up behind him. Allingham's natural imagery adds to the magical elements of his characters. A 'gizzard' is an old-fashioned word used to describe the stomach: it originally referred to part of a bird's stomach.

An Elf sat on a twig,
He was not very big,
He sang a little song,
He did not think it wrong;
But he was on a Wizard's ground,
Who hated all sweet sound.

Elf, Elf,
Take care of yourself.
He's coming behind you,
To seize you and bind you
And stifle your song.
The Wizard! The Wizard!
He changes his shape
In crawling along –
An ugly old ape,
A poisonous lizard,
A spotted spider,
A wormy glider
The Wizard! The Wizard!
He's up on the bough
He'll bite through your gizzard,
He's close to you now!

The Elf went on with his song,
It grew more clear and strong;
It lifted him into air,
He floated singing away,
With rainbows in his hair;

While the Wizard-Worm from his creep
Made a sudden leap,
Fell down into a hole,
And, ere his magic word he could say,
Was eaten up by a Mole.

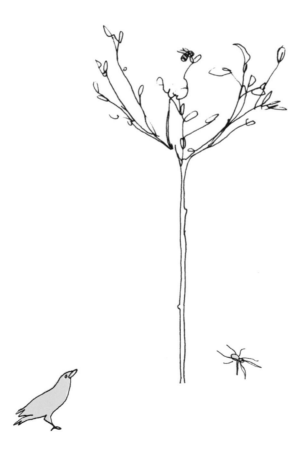

The Fly-Away Horse

EUGENE FIELD
1850–95

Oh, a wonderful horse is the Fly-Away Horse –
    Perhaps you have seen him before;
Perhaps, while you slept, his shadow has swept
    Through the moonlight that floats on the floor.
For it's only at night, when the stars twinkle bright,
    That the Fly-Away Horse, with a neigh
And a pull at his rein and a toss of his mane,
    Is up on his heels and away!
      The moon in the sky,
      As he gallopeth by,
    Cries: 'Oh! What a marvellous sight!'
      And the Stars in dismay
      Hide their faces away
      In the lap of old Grandmother Night.

It is yonder, out yonder, the Fly-Away Horse
    Speedeth ever and ever away –
Over meadows and lane, over mountains and plains,
    Over streamlets that sing at their play;
And over the sea like a ghost sweepeth he,
    While the ships they go sailing below,
And he speedeth so fast that the men on the mast
    Adjudge him some portent of woe.
      'What ho, there!' they cry,
      As he flourishes by
    With a whisk of his beautiful tail;
      And the fish in the sea
      Are as scared as can be,
      From the nautilus up to the whale!

And the Fly-Away Horse seeks those far-away lands
    You little folk dream of at night –
Where candy-trees grow, and honey-brooks flow,
    And corn-fields with popcorn are white;
And the beasts in the wood are ever so good
    To children who visit them there –
What glory astride of a lion to ride,
    Or to wrestle around with a bear!
        The monkeys, they say:
        'Come on, let us play,'
    And they frisk in the coconut-trees:
        While the parrots, that cling
        To the peanut-vines, sing
        Or converse with comparative ease!

Off! scamper to bed – you shall ride him tonight!
    For, as soon as you've fallen asleep,
With a jubilant neigh he shall bear you away
    Over forest and hillside and deep!
But tell us, my dear, all you see and you hear
    In those beautiful lands over there,
Where the Fly-Away Horse wings his far-away course
    With the wee one consigned to his care.
        Then grandma will cry
        In amazement: 'Oh, my!'
    And she'll think it could never be so;
        And only we two
        Shall know it is true –
        You and I, little precious! shall know!

Friendship and Love

Us Two

A.A. MILNE
1882–1956

Christopher Robin is the narrator of 'Us Two'; he and Winnie-the-Pooh are friends and share adventures in the Hundred Acre Wood. Winnie-the-Pooh was a real teddy bear, bought from the department store Harrods for Christopher Robin by his father, A. A. Milne. All of the characters from the Pooh books could be found in Christopher Robin's toy chest, and A.A. Milne used to make up stories about them to entertain his son. If you read 'Us Two' aloud, you hear the names 'Pooh' and 'Me' so often that the two almost join together, just as Christopher Robin and Pooh were inseparable.

Wherever I am, there's always Pooh.
There's always Pooh and Me.
Whatever I do, he wants to do,
'Where are you going today?' says Pooh:
'Well, that's very odd 'cos I was too.
Let's go together,' says Pooh, says he.
'Let's go together,' says Pooh.

'What's twice eleven?' I said to Pooh.
('Twice what?' said Pooh to Me.)
'I think it ought to be twenty-two.'
'Just what I think myself,' said Pooh.
'It wasn't an easy sum to do,
But that's what it is,' said Pooh, said he.
'That's what it is,' said Pooh.

'Let's look for dragons,' I said to Pooh.
'Yes, let's,' said Pooh to Me.
We crossed the river and found a few –
'Yes, those are dragons all right,' said Pooh.
'As soon as I saw their beaks I knew.
That's what they are,' said Pooh, said he.
'That's what they are,' said Pooh.

'Let's frighten the dragons,' I said to Pooh.
'That's right,' said Pooh to Me.
'I'm not afraid,' I said to Pooh,
And I held his paw and I shouted 'Shoo!
Silly old dragons!'– and off they flew.
'I wasn't afraid,' said Pooh, said he,
'I'm never afraid with you.'

So wherever I am, there's always Pooh,
There's always Pooh and Me.
'What would I do?' I said to Pooh,
'If it wasn't for you,' and Pooh said: 'True,
It isn't much fun for One, but Two
Can stick together,' says Pooh, says he.
'That's how it is,' says Pooh.

Rainbows

KHALIL GIBRAN
1883–1931

If I could catch a rainbow
I would do it just for you.
And share with you its beauty
On the days you're feeling blue.

If I could build a mountain
You could call your very own.
A place to find serenity
A place to be alone.

If I could take your troubles
I would toss them in the sea.
But all these things I'm finding
Are impossible for me,

I cannot build a mountain
Or catch a rainbow fair
But let me be . . . what I know best,
A friend that's always there.

An Old English Riddle

ANON

This riddle is over a thousand years old and it is written in Old English. English has changed a lot since then, but you might recognise some of the words, like 'wundor' (wonder) and 'wordum' (words). If you want to try reading this out loud, ð and þ are both the same as our 'th' sound, so 'Moððe' is just the same as 'Moth'! Old English uses a lot of alliteration, (look at the 'w' words in the second line) and is written with a caesura (a break) in the middle of each line. What do you think the riddle is describing? (The answer is below.)

Moððe word fræt.   Me þæt þuhte
wrætlicu wyrd,   þa ic þæt wundor gefrægn,
þæt se wyrm   forswealg wera gied sumes,
þeof in þystro   þrymfæstne cwide
and þæs strangan staþol.   Stalgiest ne wæs
wihte þe gleawra,   þe he þam wordum swealg.

Translation
A moth ate words. To me that seemed
A strange event, when I heard about it, a wonder;
That the worm swallowed the words of some man,
A thief in darkness, a glorious speech,
And its firm foundation. The thief-guest was none
The wiser, after he swallowed the words!

Answer: A bookworm, which is a little insect that likes to eat books.

The Duck and the Kangaroo

EDWARD LEAR
1812–88

Said the Duck to the Kangaroo,
    'Good gracious! how you hop!
Over the fields and the water too,
    As if you never would stop!
My life is a bore in this nasty pond,
And I long to go out in the world beyond!
    I wish I could hop like you!'
    Said the Duck to the Kangaroo.

'Please give me a ride on your back!'
    Said the Duck to the Kangaroo.
'I would sit quite still, and say nothing but "Quack,"
    The whole of the long day through!
And we'd go to the Dee, and the Jelly Bo Lee,
Over the land, and over the sea; –
    Please take me a ride! O do!'
    Said the Duck to the Kangaroo.

Said the Kangaroo to the Duck,
    'This requires some little reflection;
Perhaps on the whole it might bring me luck,
    And there seems but one objection,
Which is, if you'll let me speak so bold,
Your feet are unpleasantly wet and cold,
    And would probably give me the roo-
    Matiz!' said the Kangaroo.

Said the Duck, 'As I sate on the rocks,
    I have thought over that completely,
And I bought four pairs of worsted socks
    Which fit my web-feet neatly.
And to keep out the cold I've bought a cloak,
And every day a cigar I'll smoke,
    All to follow my own dear true
    Love of a Kangaroo!'

Said the Kangaroo, 'I'm ready!
    All in the moonlight pale;
But to balance me well, dear Duck, sit steady!
    And quite at the end of my tail!'
So away they went with a hop and a bound,
And they hopped the whole world three times round;
    And who so happy, – O who,
    As the Duck and the Kangaroo?

The Girl with Many Eyes

TIM BURTON
1958–

Tim Burton is best known as a film-maker. You may have seen his films Charlie and the Chocolate Factory *and* Alice in Wonderland, *which were based on books by Roald Dahl and Lewis Carroll. Tim Burton's work is often funny, sometimes magical, and frequently makes you think from the point of view of the character in the story who is alone and may be lonely.*

One day in the park
I had quite a surprise.
I met a girl
who had many eyes.

She was really quite pretty
(and also quite shocking!)
and I noticed she had a mouth,
so we ended up talking.

We talked about flowers,
and her poetry classes,
and the problems she'd have
if she ever wore glasses.

It's great to know a girl
who has so many eyes,
but you really get wet
when she breaks down and cries.

The Arrow and the Song

H.W. LONGFELLOW
1807–82

I shot an arrow into the air,
It fell to earth, I knew not where;
For, so swiftly it flew, the sight
Could not follow it in its flight.

I breathed a song into the air,
It fell to earth, I knew not where;
For who has sight so keen and strong,
That it can follow the flight of song?

Long, long afterward, in an oak
I found the arrow, still unbroke;
And the song, from beginning to end,
I found again in the heart of a friend.

Sally in Our Alley

HENRY CAREY
1687–1743

Of all the girls that are so smart
   There's none like pretty Sally;
She is the darling of my heart,
   And she lives in our alley.
There is no lady in the land
   Is half so sweet as Sally;
She is the darling of my heart,
   And she lives in our alley.

Her father he makes cabbage-nets
   And through the streets does cry 'em;
Her mother she sells laces long
   To such as please to buy 'em;
But sure such folks could ne'er beget
   So sweet a girl as Sally!
She is the darling of my heart,
   And she lives in our alley.

When she is by, I leave my work
   (I love her so sincerely);
My master comes like any Turk
   And bangs me most severely;
But let him bang his bellyful,
   I'll bear it all for Sally;
She is the darling of my heart,
   And she lives in our alley.

Of all the days that's in the week
    I dearly love but one day –
And that's the day that comes betwixt
    A Saturday and Monday;
For then I'm dressed all in my best
    To walk abroad with Sally;
She is the darling of my heart,
    And she lives in our alley.

My master carries me to church,
    And often am I blamed
Because I leave him in the lurch
    As soon as text is named;
I leave the church in sermon-time
    And slink away to Sally;
She is the darling of my heart,
    And she lives in our alley.

When Christmas comes about again,
    O, then I shall have money;
I'll hoard it up, and box it all,
    I'll give it to my honey;
I would it were ten thousand pounds,
    I'd give it all to Sally;
She is the darling of my hearts,
    And she lives in our alley.

My master and the neighbours all
    Make game of me and Sally;
And, but for her, I'd better be
    A slave and row a galley;
But when my seven long years are out,
    O, then I'll marry Sally!
O, then we'll wed, and then we'll bed,
    But not in our alley.

Love and Friendship

EMILY BRONTË
1818–48

This poem uses similes to compare love and friendship with roses and holly. While roses in bloom are breathtaking in their beauty, holly is hardier and will be green even when the rose has withered in the winter. This implies that friendship is more reliable and enduring than love, which can blossom and die very rapidly. Like holly, friendship is 'evergreen' and can flourish when everything is bleak and cold. Emily Brontë started writing poems as a child, but she is best known for her masterpiece, the novel Wuthering Heights; *her sisters Charlotte and Anne were also extraordinarily talented, famous writers.*

Love is like the wild rose-briar,
Friendship like the holly-tree –
The holly is dark when the rose-briar blooms
But which will bloom most constantly?

The wild-rose briar is sweet in the spring,
Its summer blossoms scent the air;
Yet wait till winter comes again
And who will call the wild-briar fair?

Then scorn the silly rose-wreath now
And deck thee with the holly's sheen,
That when December blights thy brow
He may still leave thy garland green.

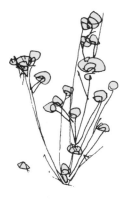

He Wishes for the Cloths of Heaven

W.B. YEATS
1865–1939

Had I the heavens' embroidered cloths,
Enwrought with golden and silver light,
The blue and the dim and the dark cloths
Of night and light and the half-light,
I would spread the cloths under your feet:
But I, being poor, have only my dreams;
I have spread my dreams under your feet;
Tread softly because you tread on my dreams.

Friendship

ELIZABETH JENNINGS
1926–2001

Such love I cannot analyse;
It does not rest in lips or eyes,
Neither in kisses nor caress.
Partly, I know, it's gentleness

And understanding in one word
Or in brief letters. It's preserved
By trust and by respect and awe.
These are the words I'm feeling for.

Two people, yes, two lasting friends.
The giving comes, the taking ends.
There is no measure for such things.
For this all Nature slows and sings.

Bright Star!

JOHN KEATS
1795–1821

Bright star! would I were steadfast as thou art –
    Not in lone splendour hung aloft the night
And watching, with eternal lids apart,
    Like nature's patient, sleepless Eremite,
The moving waters at their priestlike task
    Of pure ablution round earth's human shores,
Or gazing on the new soft-fallen mask
    Of snow upon the mountains and the moors –
No – yet still steadfast, still unchangeable,
    Pillowed upon my fair love's ripening breast,
To feel for ever its soft fall and swell,
    Awake for ever in a sweet unrest,
Still, still to hear her tender-taken breath,
    And so live ever – or else swoon to death.

She Walks in Beauty

GEORGE GORDON, LORD BYRON
1788–1824

yron was inspired to write this poem in 1814 when he glimpsed a young woman, who was his cousin by marriage, at a party, wearing a black mourning gown covered with spangles.

She walks in beauty, like the night
    Of cloudless climes and starry skies;
And all that's best of dark and bright
    Meet in her aspect and her eyes:
Thus mellowed to that tender light
    Which heaven to gaudy day denies.

One shade the more, one ray the less,
    Had half impaired the nameless grace
Which waves in every raven tress,
    Or softly lightens o'er her face;
Where thoughts serenely sweet express
    How pure, how dear their dwelling place.

And on that cheek, and o'er that brow,
    So soft, so calm, yet eloquent,
The smiles that win, the tints that glow,
    But tell of days in goodness spent,
A mind at peace with all below,
    A heart whose love is innocent!

Song: Why So Pale and Wan?

SIR JOHN SUCKLING
1609–42

*I*n this poem, Suckling mocks the fashion for young men to appear tortured by love (a common theme in both real life and poetry). We could contrast this with Keats' poem 'La Belle Dame sans Merci' (see page 165) where the forsaken lover is seriously described as 'pale . . . haggard and so woe-begone'. Suckling, however, encourages the lover not to continue to waste his time, since the woman is not interested in him. The last line, 'the devil take her', was a common expression meaning 'give up on her'.

Why so pale and wan, fond lover?
    Prithee, why so pale?
Will, when looking well can't move her,
    Looking ill prevail?
    Prithee, why so pale?

Why so dull and mute, young sinner?
    Prithee, why so mute?
Will, when speaking well can't win her,
    Saying nothing do 't?
    Prithee, why so mute?

Quit, quit, for shame, this will not move;
    This will not take her;
If of herself she will not love,
    Nothing can make her:
    The devil take her.

A Red, Red Rose

ROBERT BURNS
1759–96

*R*obert Burns was a Scottish farmer who became a celebrity as a self-taught poet. He wrote poems in standard literary English, and others, like 'A Red, Red Rose', in his own Lowland Scots dialect. He collected ballads from local sources, edited them and sent them to Pietro Urbani, a singer who set many of them to traditional Scottish melodies. 'Auld Lang Syne', which is sung on New Year's Eve, is a famous example. 'A Red, Red Rose' is an extremely well-known love poem – the first line, with its famous simile, is often quoted. Note how the poem develops and how other elements such as time passing are introduced.

> O my luve is like a red, red rose,
> That's newly sprung in June:
> O my luve's like the melodie,
> That's sweetly play'd in tune.
> As fair art thou, my bonnie lass,
> So deep in luve am I;
> And I will luve thee still, my dear,
> Till a' the seas gang dry.
>
> Till a' the seas gang dry, my dear,
> And the rocks melt wi' the sun!
> And I will luve thee still, my dear,
> While the sands o' life shall run.
> And fare-thee-weel, my only luve,
> And fare-thee-weel a while!
> And I will come again, my luve,
> Tho' it were ten-thousand mile.

How Do I Love Thee?

ELIZABETH BARRETT BROWNING
1806–61

'How do I Love Thee?' is the best-known poem in Elizabeth Barrett's collection *Sonnets from the Portuguese*, published in 1850. They reflect her love for her husband, the poet Robert Browning; the pair had eloped in a blaze of publicity in 1846. Publishing the collection under the disguise of Portuguese translations helped conceal how personal the poems were. Browning used the pet name of 'my little Portuguese' to refer to Elizabeth. The sonnet uses anaphora, a poetical term for repetition; each line counts another 'way' in which Elizabeth can describe her love. She switches from rather exalted, grandiose claims to images of their 'everyday' partnership, allowing the reader to appreciate the emotional range of her love.

How do I love thee? Let me count the ways.
I love thee to the depth and breadth and height
My soul can reach, when feeling out of sight
For the ends of Being and ideal Grace.
I love thee to the level of everyday's
Most quiet need, by sun and candle-light.
I love thee freely, as men strive for Right:
I love thee purely, as they turn from Praise.
I love thee with the passion put to use
In my old griefs, and with my childhood's faith.
I love thee with a love I seemed to lose
With my lost saints! – I love thee with the breath,
Smiles, tears, of all my life! – and, if God choose,
I shall but love thee better after death.

Sonnet 18

WILLIAM SHAKESPEARE
1564–1616

The Shakespearean (or English) sonnet has a rhyme scheme 'ababcdcdefefgg' and is composed of three quatrains and a final couplet. Many phrases from this well-known sonnet, one of 154 written by Shakespeare, have entered common usage, from its opening line to the 'darling buds of May'. The sonnet's popularity has ensured that its last lines, 'So long lives this, and this gives life to thee', are indeed true: Shakespeare's beloved lives on through the words of the poem.

Shall I compare thee to a Summer's day?
Thou art more lovely and more temperate:
Rough winds do shake the darling buds of May,
And Summer's lease hath all too short a date:
Sometime too hot the eye of heaven shines,
And often is his gold complexion dimm'd;
And every fair from fair sometime declines,
By chance or nature's changing course untrimm'd:
But thy eternal Summer shall not fade
Nor lose possession of that fair thou owest;
Nor shall Death brag thou wanderest in his shade,
When in eternal lines to time thou growest:
    So long as men can breathe, or eyes can see,
    So long lives this, and this gives life to thee.

Love

GEORGE HERBERT

1593–1633

*L*ove is personified in this poem, becoming the person with whom the narrator is having a conversation. The narrator is a diffident character who feels unworthy of engaging with Love, and turns to leave, ashamed. But he is beckoned in to enjoy Love's hospitality. Love is addressed as 'Lord', just as God would be traditionally addressed in Christian poetry or verse. We think this is a wonderful poem because it suggests the gentleness and humility of love and how it is open to us all.

Love bade me welcome, yet my soul drew back,
    Guilty of dust and sin.
But quick-ey'd Love, observing me grow slack
    From my first entrance in,
Drew nearer to me, sweetly questioning
    If I lack'd anything.

'A guest,' I answer'd, 'worthy to be here';
    Love said, 'You shall be he.'
'I, the unkind, the ungrateful? Ah my dear,
    I cannot look on thee.'
Love took my hand and smiling did reply,
    'Who made the eyes but I?'

'Truth, Lord, but I have marr'd them: let my shame
    Go where it doth deserve.'
'And know you not,' says Love, 'who bore the blame?'
    'My dear, then I will serve.'
'You must sit down,' says Love, 'and taste my meat.'
    So I did sit and eat.

La Belle Dame sans Merci

JOHN KEATS
1795–1821

The title of this poem is in French and it means 'The Beautiful Lady without Pity'. John Keats writes about a knight who is in love with a 'faery' woman, and imitates poetry written in medieval times, when much was written about fairies. He dashed this poem off and included it in a letter to his brother, George. Although it is now one of his most famous poems, Keats never considered it to be one of his best.

O what can ail thee, knight-at-arms,
 Alone and palely loitering?
The sedge has wither'd from the lake,
 And no birds sing.

O what can ail thee, knight-at-arms!
 So haggard and so woe-begone?
The squirrel's granary is full,
 And the harvest's done.

I see a lily on thy brow
 With anguish moist and fever dew,
And on thy cheeks a fading rose
 Fast withereth too.

I met a lady in the meads,
 Full beautiful – a faery's child,
Her hair was long, her foot was light,
 And her eyes were wild.

I made a garland for her head,
 And bracelets too, and fragrant zone;
She look'd at me as she did love,
 And made sweet moan.

I set her on my pacing steed,
  And nothing else saw all day long,
For sidelong would she bend, and sing
  A faery's song.

She found me roots of relish sweet,
  And honey wild, and manna-dew,
And sure in language strange she said –
  'I love thee true.'

She took me to her elfin grot,
  And there she wept, and sigh'd full sore,
And there I shut her wild wild eyes
  With kisses four.

And there she lulled me asleep
  And there I dream'd – Ah! woe betide!
The latest dream I ever dream'd
  On the cold hill's side.

I saw pale kings and princes too,
  Pale warriors, death-pale were they all;
They cried – 'La Belle Dame sans Merci
  Hath thee in thrall!'

I saw their starved lips in the gloam,
  With horrid warning gaped wide,
And I awoke and found me here,
  On the cold hill's side.

And this is why I sojourn here,
  Alone and palely loitering,
Though the sedge is wither'd from the lake,
  And no birds sing.

The Chilterns

RUPERT BROOKE
1887–1915

Rupert Brooke uses the landscape to reflect his narrator's emotional condition; the narrator has parted from a girl, and he employs the image of the open road to show how he must journey on regardless. Brooke uses 'pathetic fallacy' (whereby human feelings are given to objects or to nature – in this case, the weather) to show the mixture of emotions he feels towards the relationship that has just ended – the joy of the sun and the 'sharp sting' of rain.

Your hands, my dear, adorable,
    Your lips of tenderness
– Oh, I've loved you faithfully and well,
    Three years, or a bit less.
    It wasn't a success.

Thank God, that's done! and I'll take the road,
    Quit of my youth and you,
The Roman road to Wendover
    By Tring and Lilley Hoo,
    As a free man may do.

For youth goes over, the joys that fly,
    The tears that follow fast;
And the dirtiest things we do must lie
    Forgotten at the last;
    Even Love goes past.

What's left behind I shall not find,
    The splendour and the pain;
The splash of sun, the shouting wind,
    And the brave sting of rain,
    I may not meet again.

But the years, that take the best away,
　　Give something in the end;
And a better friend than love have they,
　　For none to mar or mend,
　　That have themselves to friend.

I shall desire and I shall find
　　The best of my desires;
The autumn road, the mellow wind
　　That soothes the darkening shires.
　　And laughter, and inn-fires.

White mist about the black hedgerows,
　　The slumbering Midland plain,
The silence where the clover grows,
　　And the dead leaves in the lane,
　　Certainly, these remain.

And I shall find some girl perhaps,
　　And a better one than you,
With eyes as wise, but kindlier,
　　And lips as soft, but true.
　　And I daresay she will do.

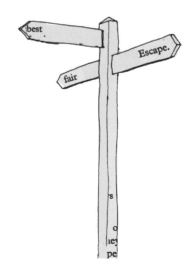

We'll Go No More A-Roving

GEORGE GORDON, LORD BYRON
1788–1824

Lord Byron uses the poetic technique of assonance, with the long 'o' sounds in the first line creating a moaning effect to convey how tired he is. Look for his use of sibilance (a repeated 's' sound) in the first line of the second verse, 'For the sword outwears its sheath', which suggests listlessness and fatigue. Byron included this 1817 poem in a letter he wrote to a friend to describe his feeling of exhaustion and despondency. He led a flamboyant, romantic life, and this poem reflects the notion that too much pleasure can lead to trouble. The phrase 'a-roving' is a feature of the traditional sea-songs Byron would have known.

So we'll go no more a-roving
   So late into the night,
Though the heart be still as loving,
   And the moon be still as bright.

For the sword outwears its sheath,
   And the soul wears out the breast,
And the heart must pause to breathe,
   And love itself have rest.

Though the night was made for loving,
   And the day returns too soon,
Yet we'll go no more a-roving
   By the light of the moon.

Animals, Nature and Seasons

Ducks' Ditty

KENNETH GRAHAME
1859–1932

A ditty is a short, simple poem that is easy to remember, often sung to a catchy tune. The character Ratty composes this poem while sitting on the river bank in Kenneth Grahame's book The Wind in the Willows: *he enjoys writing poetry in reflective moments, but often has difficulty finding inspiration.*

All along the backwater,
Through the rushes tall,
Ducks are a-dabbling,
Up tails all!

Ducks' tails, drakes' tails,
Yellow feet a-quiver,
Yellow bills all out of sight
Busy in the river!

Slushy green undergrowth
Where the roach swim –
Here we keep our larder,
Cool and full and dim!

Every one for what he likes!
We like to be
Heads down, tails up,
Dabbling free!

High in the blue above
Swifts whirl and call –
We are down a-dabbling
Up tails all!

Mary's Lamb

SARAH JOSEPHA HALE
1788–1879

Sarah Josepha Hale was inspired to write this poem by her pet lamb, which she took to school one day. Thomas Edison, who invented the phonograph (an early record-player), chose this poem as his first ever recording. William Blake treats the lamb very differently, as a symbol of purity and gentleness rather than a familiar pet – see page 181.

Mary had a little lamb,
Its fleece was white as snow.
And everywhere that Mary went,
The lamb was sure to go;
He followed her to school one day –
That was against the rule,
It made the children laugh and play
To see a lamb at school.

And so the teacher turned him out,
But still he lingered near,
And waited patiently about,
Till Mary did appear.
And then he ran to her and laid
His head upon her arm,
As if he said, 'I'm not afraid –
You'll shield me from all harm.'

'What makes the lamb love Mary so?'
The little children cry;
'Oh, Mary loves the lamb, you know,'
The teacher did reply,
'And you each gentle animal
In confidence may bind,
And make it follow at your call,
If you are always kind.'

Pussy can sit by the fire and sing

RUDYARD KIPLING

1865–1936

This poem tells the story of the selfish cat versus the faithful dog. The poem appears in the story 'The Cat that Walked by Himself', which comes from the Just So Stories, *one of Rudyard Kipling's most famous works.*

Pussy can sit by the fire and sing,
　　Pussy can climb a tree,
Or play with a silly old cork and string
　　To 'muse herself, not me.
But *I* like *Binkie* my dog, because
　　He knows how to behave;
So, *Binkie*'s the same as the First Friend was,
　　And I am the Man in the Cave.

Pussy will play Man-Friday till
　　It's time to wet her paw
And make her walk on the window-sill
　　(For the footprint Crusoe saw);
Then she fluffles her tail and mews,
　　And scratches and won't attend.
But *Binkie* will play whatever I choose,
　　And he is my true First Friend!

Pussy will rub my knees with her head
　　Pretending she loves me hard;
But the very minute I go to my bed
　　Pussy runs out in the yard,
And there she stays till the morning-light;
　　So I know it is only pretend;
But *Binkie*, he snores at my feet all night,
　　And he is my Firstest Friend!

The Cow

ROBERT LOUIS STEVENSON
1850–94

The friendly cow, all red and white,
    I love with all my heart:
She gives me cream with all her might,
    To eat with apple-tart.

She wanders lowing here and there,
    And yet she cannot stray,
All in the pleasant open air,
    The pleasant light of day;

And blown by all the winds that pass
    And wet with all the showers,
She walks among the meadow grass
    And eats the meadow flowers.

Snow Flakes

EMILY DICKINSON
1830–86

I counted till they danced so
Their slippers leaped the town –
And then I took a pencil
To note the rebels down –
And then they grew so jolly
I did resign the prig –
And ten of my once stately toes
Are marshalled for a jig!

The Crocodile

LEWIS CARROLL
1832–98

Alice recites this poem in Alice in Wonderland. *She begins by reciting 'How doth the little busy bee', a typically didactic Isaac Watts poem, with a moral concerning the value of hard work, then switches to this poem about a crocodile, which has no moral purpose. She celebrates the cunning of the 'little crocodile', poking fun at the original Watts poem. Lewis Carroll's parody has become far more famous than the poem that inspired it.*

How doth the little crocodile
  Improve his shining tail,
And pour the waters of the Nile
  On every golden scale!

How cheerfully he seems to grin,
  How neatly spread his claws,
And welcomes little fishes in
  With gently smiling jaws!

The African Lion

A.E. HOUSMAN
1859–1936

This poem contains a lesson: the lion only eats naughty boys. The poem is in the tradition of Aesop's Fables *and the cautionary tales of Hilaire Belloc, such as 'Matilda, Who Told Lies and Was Burned to Death' on page 70. A.E. Housman was best known for writing serious poems and for being a superb classical scholar and critic. His most famous work is* A Shropshire Lad.

To meet a bad lad on the African waste
    Is a thing that a lion enjoys;
But he rightly and strongly objects to the taste
    Of good and uneatable boys.

When he bites off a piece of a boy of that sort
    He spits it right out of his mouth,
And retires with a loud and dissatisfied snort
    To the east, or the west, or the south.

So lads of good habits, on coming across
    A lion, need feel no alarm
For they know they are sure to escape with the loss
    Of a leg, or a head, or an arm.

The Cricket

KOBAYASHI ISSA
1763–1827

*I*n the seventeenth century, a Japanese poet named Bashō (1644–94) developed the haiku: a short poem, just three lines long, which usually celebrates a wonder of nature. It does not rhyme but has strict rules: the first and third lines have five syllables and the middle line has seven. Today, English-language haikus experiment with the traditional form and are not so strict with their syllable count. Here is a haiku, which does not follow the rules, by Issa, one of Japan's most prolific haiku writers. He wrote 20,000 poems.

> I'm going to roll over,
> So please move,
> Cricket.

The Eagle

ALFRED, LORD TENNYSON
1809–92

> He clasps the crag with crooked hands;
> Close to the sun in lonely lands,
> Ring'd with the azure world, he stands.
>
> The wrinkled sea beneath him crawls;
> He watches from his mountain walls,
> And like a thunderbolt he falls.

Amulet

TED HUGHES
1930–98

Ted Hughes loved animals and wrote many poems about them. An amulet is an object (in this case a wolf's fang) that is hung on a string around its owner's neck to give magical protection. Hughes imagines how the wolf's fang connects with the rest of nature in a circle. In the final line, Hughes brings the circle back to the beginning.

Inside the wolf's fang, the mountain of heather.
Inside the mountain of heather, the wolf's fur.
Inside the wolf's fur, the ragged forest.
Inside the ragged forest, the wolf's foot.
Inside the wolf's foot, the stony horizon.
Inside the stony horizon, the wolf's tongue.
Inside the wolf's tongue, the doe's tears.
Inside the doe's tears, the frozen swamp.
Inside the frozen swamp, the wolf's blood.
Inside the wolf's blood, the snow wind.
Inside the snow wind, the wolf's eye.
Inside the wolf's eye, the North star.
Inside the North star, the wolf's fang.

The Donkey

G.K. CHESTERTON
1874–1936

The narrator of this poem is a donkey recalling his hour of triumph bearing Jesus into Jerusalem, an event recorded in the New Testament. The final lines refer to the jubilant crowd hurling palm leaves into Jesus's path. Christians still commemorate this today on Palm Sunday. In the middle stanzas, the donkey admits his own ugliness and insignificance. However, this may explain why Jesus chose to ride him.

When fishes flew and forests walked
    And figs grew upon thorn,
Some moment when the moon was blood
    Then surely I was born;

With monstrous head and sickening cry
    And ears like errant wings,
The devil's walking parody
    On all four-footed things.

The tattered outlaw of the earth,
    Of ancient crooked will;
Starve, scourge, deride me: I am dumb,
    I keep my secret still.

Fools! For I also had my hour;
    One far fierce hour and sweet:
There was a shout about my ears,
    And palms before my feet.

The Lamb

WILLIAM BLAKE
1757–1827

This poem, taken from the 1789 collection Songs of Innocence, *explores the wonder of creation using the Christian symbol of the Lamb – Jesus was called the 'Lamb of God' in the New Testament. It is a companion poem to 'The Tyger', which follows.*

Little Lamb, who made thee?
　Dost thou know who made thee?
Gave thee life, and bid thee feed
By the stream and o'er the mead;
Gave thee clothing of delight,
Softest clothing, woolly, bright;
Gave thee such a tender voice,
Making all the vales rejoice?
　Little Lamb, who made thee?
　Dost thou know who made thee?

Little Lamb, I'll tell thee,
　Little Lamb, I'll tell thee:
He is called by thy name,
For he calls himself a Lamb.
He is meek, and he is mild;
He became a little child.
I a child, and thou a lamb,
We are called by his name.
　Little Lamb, God bless thee!
　Little Lamb, God bless thee!

The Tyger

WILLIAM BLAKE

1757–1827

'The Tyger' was published five years after 'The Lamb' in Songs of Experience; William Blake's narrator seems astonished that the same Creator who 'framed' (created) the meek and gentle lamb is also responsible for the menacing tyger. Blake explicitly identified God as the lamb's creator, but he ends this poem questioning who can possibly have created such a fearsome animal.

Tyger! Tyger! burning bright
In the forests of the night
What immortal hand or eye
Could frame thy fearful symmetry?

In what distant deeps or skies
Burnt the fire of thine eyes?
On what wings dare he aspire?
What the hand dare seize the fire?

And what shoulder, and what art,
Could twist the sinews of thy heart?
And when thy heart began to beat,
What dread hand? and what dread feet?

What the hammer? what the chain?
In what furnace was thy brain?
What the anvil? what dread grasp
Dare its deadly terrors clasp?

When the stars threw down their spears,
And water'd heaven with their tears,
Did He smile his work to see?
Did He who made the Lamb make thee?

Tyger! Tyger! burning bright
In the forests of the night,
What immortal hand or eye
Dare frame thy fearful symmetry?

The Rainbow

CHRISTINA ROSSETTI
1830–94

Boats sail on the rivers,
    And ships sail on the seas;
But clouds that sail across the sky
    Are prettier than these.

There are bridges on the rivers,
    As pretty as you please;
But the bow that bridges heaven,
    And overtops the trees,
And builds a road from earth to sky,
    Is prettier far than these.

Sea Fever

JOHN MASEFIELD
1878–1967

In this poem John Masefield looks back with fondness at the life he led as a sailor. He now misses the companionship that he found as part of a ship's crew.

I must go down to the seas again, to the lonely sea and the sky,
And all I ask is a tall ship and a star to steer her by,
And the wheel's kick and the wind's song and the white sail's shaking,
And a grey mist on the sea's face and a grey dawn breaking.

I must go down to the seas again, for the call of the running tide
Is a wild call and a clear call that may not be denied;
And all I ask is a windy day with the white clouds flying,
And the flung spray and the blown spume, and the sea-gulls crying.

I must go down to the seas again, to the vagrant gypsy life,
To the gull's way and the whale's way where the wind's like a whetted knife;
And all I ask is a merry yarn from a laughing fellow-rover,
And quiet sleep and a sweet dream when the long trick's over.

A Boat, Beneath a Sunny Sky

LEWIS CARROLL
1832–98

This poem is by Lewis Carroll, who was inspired to write Alice in Wonderland *by a girl called Alice Pleasance Liddell. He uses the first letter of each line to spell out her name, thereby creating an acrostic poem.*

A boat, beneath a sunny sky
Lingering onward dreamily
In an evening of July –

Children three that nestle near,
Eager eye and willing ear,
Pleased a simple tale to hear –

Long has paled that sunny sky:
Echoes fade and memories die:
Autumn frosts have slain July.

Still she haunts me, phantomwise,
Alice moving under skies
Never seen by waking eyes.

Children yet, the tale to hear,
Eager eye and willing ear,
Lovingly shall nestle near.

In a Wonderland they lie,
Dreaming as the days go by,
Dreaming as the summers die:

Ever drifting down the stream –
Lingering in the golden gleam –
Life, what is it but a dream?

Pied Beauty

GERARD MANLEY HOPKINS
1844–89

As a boy, Hopkins was terribly stubborn. He once bet a school friend that he could last without water for three weeks and only gave in after collapsing, with a blackened tongue. He grew up to be a deeply religious man who saw a world 'charged with the grandeur of God'. This poem shows the degree to which Hopkins saw God as responsible for even the smallest miracles of creation – the pink flecks on a trout or the sky coloured like a 'brinded' (or spotted) cow. Hopkins moves from praising this glorious variety to insisting that God's own beauty is unchanging. The poem ends with the simple instruction to 'Praise him'.

Glory be to God for dappled things –
   For skies of couple-colour as a brinded cow;
     For rose-moles all in stipple upon trout that swim;
Fresh-firecoal chestnut-falls; finches' wings;
   Landscape plotted and pieced – fold, fallow, and plough;
     And áll trádes, their gear and tackle and trim.

All things counter, original, spare, strange;
   Whatever is fickle, freckled (who knows how?)
     With swift, slow; sweet, sour; adazzle, dim;
He fathers-forth whose beauty is past change:
            Praise him.

A Boy's Song

JAMES HOGG
1770–1835

*James Hogg spent years as a boy working as a shepherd in the Scottish Borders,
so he knew the countryside well. 'Lea' is an old-fashioned word for field.*

Where the pools are bright and deep
Where the grey trout lies asleep
Up the river and o'er the lea
That's the way for Billy and me

Where the blackbird sings the latest
Where the hawthorn blooms the sweetest
Where the nestlings plentiest be
That's the way for Billy and me

Where the mowers mow the cleanest
Where the hay lies thick and greenest
There to trace the homeward bee
That's the way for Billy and me

Where the poplar grows the smallest
Where the old pine waves the tallest
Pies and rooks know who we are
That's the way for Billy and me

Where the hazel bank is steepest
Where the shadow falls the deepest
Where the clustering nuts fall free
That's the way for Billy and me

Why the boys should drive away
Little sweet maidens from the play
Or love to banter and fight so well
That's the thing I never could tell

But this I know, I love to play
Through the meadow, among the hay
Up the water and over the lea
That's the way for Billy and me

The Lake Isle of Innisfree

W.B. YEATS
1865–1939

I will arise and go now, and go to Innisfree,
And a small cabin build there, of clay and wattles made;
Nine bean-rows will I have there, a hive for the honey-bee,
And live alone in the bee-loud glade.

And I shall have some peace there, for peace comes dropping slow,
Dropping from the veils of the morning to where the cricket sings;
There midnight's all a glimmer, and noon a purple glow,
And evening full of the linnet's wings.

I will arise and go now, for always night and day
I hear lake water lapping with low sounds by the shore;
While I stand on the roadway, or on the pavements grey,
I hear it in the deep heart's core.

Ode to a Nightingale

JOHN KEATS
1795–1821

One of the most famous of all Romantic poems, 'Ode to a Nightingale' typifies the use by Romantic poets of rich and sumptuous language to describe nature. The poem was apparently inspired by the song of a nightingale which Keats heard in the garden of the house where he was living in Hampstead, London. The song is a metaphor for the eternal nature of art; the 'wings of Poesy' represent timeless freedom. A major theme of Romantic poetry is the ability to find inspiration from nature, and Keats's work makes the important observation that art lives long after the death of its creator.

My heart aches, and a drowsy numbness pains
My sense, as though of hemlock I had drunk,
Or emptied some dull opiate to the drains
One minute past, and Lethe-wards had sunk:
'Tis not through envy of thy happy lot,
But being too happy in thine happiness,
That thou, light-wingèd Dryad of the trees,
In some melodious plot
Of beechen green, and shadows numberless,
Singest of summer in full-throated ease.

O for a draught of vintage! that hath been
Cool'd a long age in the deep-delvèd earth,
Tasting of Flora and the country-green,
Dance, and Provençal song, and sunburnt mirth!
O for a beaker full of the warm South!
Full of the true, the blushful Hippocrene,
With beaded bubbles winking at the brim,
And purple-stainèd mouth;
That I might drink, and leave the world unseen,
And with thee fade away into the forest dim:

Fade far away, dissolve, and quite forget
What thou among the leaves hast never known,
The weariness, the fever, and the fret
Here, where men sit and hear each other groan;
Where palsy shakes a few, sad, last grey hairs,
Where youth grows pale, and spectre-thin, and dies;
Where but to think is to be full of sorrow
And leaden-eyed despairs;
Where beauty cannot keep her lustrous eyes,
Or new Love pine at them beyond to-morrow.

Away! away! for I will fly to thee,
Not charioted by Bacchus and his pards,
But on the viewless wings of Poesy,
Though the dull brain perplexes and retards:
Already with thee! tender is the night,
And haply the Queen-Moon is on her throne,
Cluster'd around by all her starry Fays
But here there is no light,
Save what from heaven is with the breezes blown
Through verdurous glooms and winding mossy ways.

I cannot see what flowers are at my feet,
Nor what soft incense hangs upon the boughs,
But, in embalmèd darkness, guess each sweet
Wherewith the seasonable month endows
The grass, the thicket, and the fruit-tree wild;
White hawthorn, and the pastoral eglantine;
Fast-fading violets cover'd up in leaves;
And mid-May's eldest child,
The coming musk-rose, full of dewy wine,
The murmurous haunt of flies on summer eves.

Darkling I listen; and, for many a time
I have been half in love with easeful Death,
Call'd him soft names in many a musèd rhyme,
To take into the air my quiet breath;
Now more than ever seems it rich to die,
To cease upon the midnight with no pain,
While thou art pouring forth thy soul abroad
In such an ecstasy! Still wouldst thou sing, and I have ears in vain
To thy high requiem become a sod.

Thou wast not born for death, immortal Bird!
No hungry generations tread thee down;
The voice I hear this passing night was heard
In ancient days by emperor and clown:
Perhaps the self-same song that found a path
Through the sad heart of Ruth, when, sick for home,
She stood in tears amid the alien corn;
The same that ofttimes hath
Charm'd magic casements, opening on the foam
Of perilous seas, in faery lands forlorn.

Forlorn! the very word is like a bell
To toll me back from thee to my sole self!
Adieu! the fancy cannot cheat so well
As she is famed to do, deceiving elf.
Adieu! adieu! thy plaintive anthem fades
Past the near meadows, over the still stream,
Up the hill-side; and now 'tis buried deep
In the next valley-glades:
Was it a vision, or a waking dream?
Fled is that music: do I wake or sleep?

I Wandered Lonely as a Cloud

WILLIAM WORDSWORTH
1770–1850

'I wandered lonely as a cloud' is one of the most famous lines in all poetry, and this poem (also incorrectly known as 'Daffodils') is a good example of how the Romantic poets focused on nature. Alone with his thoughts, the poet is in a 'pensive mood' and connects with nature to reassure himself that life has meaning. The poem was most likely inspired by a walk Wordsworth took with his sister in the Lake District. She was also a writer and kept a regular journal: her account of that walk and the beautiful field of daffodils is similar to the finished poem. Wordsworth's wife wrote two lines of the poem, and this sense of collaboration between the poet, his sister, Dorothy, and his wife reflects the harmony that Wordsworth saw in the natural world.

I wandered lonely as a cloud
That floats on high o'er vales and hills,
When all at once I saw a crowd,
A host, of golden daffodils;
Beside the lake, beneath the trees,
Fluttering and dancing in the breeze.

Continuous as the stars that shine
And twinkle on the Milky Way,
They stretched in never-ending line
Along the margin of a bay:
Ten thousand saw I at a glance,
Tossing their heads in sprightly dance.

The waves beside them danced, but they
Out-did the sparkling waves in glee:
A poet could not but be gay,
In such a jocund company:
I gazed – and gazed – but little thought
What wealth the show to me had brought:

For oft, when on my couch I lie
In vacant or in pensive mood,
They flash upon that inward eye
Which is the bliss of solitude;
And then my heart with pleasure fills,
And dances with the daffodils.

The Trees

PHILIP LARKIN
1922–85

The trees are coming into leaf
Like something almost being said;
The recent buds relax and spread,
Their greenness is a kind of grief.

Is it that they are born again
And we grow old? No, they die too.
Their yearly trick of looking new
Is written down in rings of grain.

Yet still the unresting castles thresh
In fullgrown thickness every May.
Last year is dead, they seem to say,
Begin afresh, afresh, afresh.

Adlestrop

EDWARD THOMAS
1878–1917

An unexpected stop on a train journey makes Edward Thomas notice the beauty of the countryside in a small town he otherwise would have passed straight through. The enjambment (when the meaning continues over one line and into the next without punctuation) creates the momentum of both the poet's ongoing train journey, and nature's continuing cycle.

Yes. I remember Adlestrop –
The name, because one afternoon
Of heat the express-train drew up there
Unwontedly. It was late June.

The steam hissed. Some one cleared his throat.
No one left and no one came
On the bare platform. What I saw
Was Adlestrop – only the name

And willows, willow-herb, and grass,
And meadowsweet, and haycocks dry,
No whit less still and lonely fair
Than the high cloudlets in the sky.

And for that minute a blackbird sang
Close by, and round him, mistier,
Farther and farther, all the birds
Of Oxfordshire and Gloucestershire.

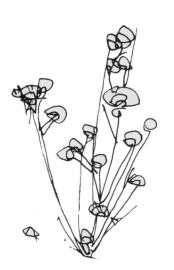

Blackberry-Picking

For Philip Hobsbaum

SEAMUS HEANEY

*Seamus Heaney brilliantly evokes the sights and sounds of the month of August by
using many densely packed verbs and adjectives. We are made to feel the same 'lust'
for the berries that leads the children to pick too many blackberries year after year. Heaney's
use of images of 'blood' and 'eyes' makes the blackberries seem alive.*

Late August, given heavy rain and sun
For a full week, the blackberries would ripen.
At first, just one, a glossy purple clot
Among others, red, green, hard as a knot.
You ate that first one and its flesh was sweet
Like thickened wine: summer's blood was in it
Leaving stains upon the tongue and lust for
Picking. Then red ones inked up and that hunger
Sent us out with milk cans, pea tins, jam pots
Where briars scratched and wet grass bleached our boots.
Round hayfields, cornfields and potato-drills
We trekked and picked until the cans were full,
Until the tickling bottom had been covered
With green ones, and on top big dark blobs burned
Like a plate of eyes. Our hands were peppered
With thorn pricks, our palms sticky as Bluebeard's.

We hoarded the fresh berries in the byre.
But when the bath was filled we found a fur,
A rat-grey fungus, glutting on our cache.
The juice was stinking too. Once off the bush
The fruit fermented, the sweet flesh would turn sour.
I always felt like crying. It wasn't fair
That all the lovely canfuls smelt of rot.
Each year I hoped they'd keep, knew they would not.

Robin Redbreast

WILLIAM ALLINGHAM
1824–89

Goodbye, goodbye to summer!
    For summer's nearly done;
The garden smiling faintly,
    Cool breezes in the sun;
Our thrushes now are silent,
    Our swallows flown away, –
But Robin's here, in coat of brown,
    With ruddy breast-knot gay.
Robin, Robin Redbreast,
    O Robin dear!
Robin singing sweetly
    In the falling of the year.

Bright yellow, red, and orange,
    The leaves come down in hosts;
The trees are Indian Princes,
    But soon they'll turn to Ghosts;
The scanty pears and apples
    Hang russet on the bough,
It's autumn, autumn, autumn late,
    'Twill soon be winter now.
Robin, Robin Redbreast,
    O Robin dear!
And welaway! My Robin,
    For pinching times are near.

The fireside for the cricket,
    The wheatsack for the mouse,
When trembling night-winds whistle
    And moan all round the house;

The frosty ways like iron,
    The branches plumed with snow, –
Alas! in winter, dead, and dark,
    Where can poor Robin go?
Robin, Robin Redbreast,
    O Robin dear!
And a crumb of bread for Robin,
    His little heart to cheer.

Trees

SARA COLERIDGE
1802–52

This didactic poem (by the daughter of Samuel Taylor Coleridge) was designed to help children learn the characteristics of some of Britain's indigenous trees.

The Oak is called the king of trees,
The Aspen quivers in the breeze,
The Poplar grows up straight and tall,
The Peach tree spreads along the wall,
The Sycamore gives pleasant shade,
The Willow droops in watery glade,
The Fir tree useful in timber gives,
The Beech amid the forest lives.

War, History and Death

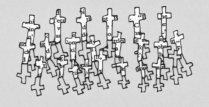

Remember, Remember the Fifth of November

ANON

This rhyme is often repeated on 5 November, also known as Bonfire Night in Britain, remembering the story of the Gunpowder Plot. Guy Fawkes, a spy and Catholic activist, was arrested on 5 November 1605 while attempting to blow up the Houses of Parliament and kill the Protestant King James I. Fawkes' story is used to show the disastrous consequences of plotting treason, and the rhyme warns us 'remember, remember' the fate of Guy Fawkes. Each year, effigies of Guy Fawkes are thrown onto bonfires, preserving a 400-year-old tradition. Fawkes met a different, but equally grisly death: he was hanged, drawn and quartered.

Remember, remember the fifth of November
  Gunpowder, treason and plot.
I see no reason
Why gunpowder treason
  Should ever be forgot.

Here Dead We Lie

A.E. HOUSMAN
1859–1936

Housman insisted that poetry should appeal to the emotions rather than the intellect, and this short poem about the First World War does just that. It uses irony to convey a bitter message about the young lives wasted in the service of honour and victory. Irony is a technique particularly suited to war poetry, because it relies upon a contradiction between words and emotions. When Housman says that 'life . . . is nothing much to lose', he clearly implies the opposite.

Here dead we lie because we did not choose
To live and shame the land from which we sprung.
Life, to be sure, is nothing much to lose,
But young men think it is, and we were young.

An Epitaph

JOHN DRYDEN
1631–1700

'Epitaph' comes from the Greek word 'epitaphion', which means a speech at a tomb. It is most often a short verse or phrase, written on the headstone over someone's grave. Epitaphs can range from comforting words, designed to reassure those who are left behind, to descriptions of the person commemorated.

Here lies my wife: here let her lie!
Now she's at rest, and so am I.

Rhyme to Remember Kings and Queens

ANON

This poem, which must date from the twentieth century, helps us remember the names of the kings and queens of England and Scotland and will give you a head start in history! It contains clues to the character of these monarchs. For example, 'Dick the Bad' refers to Richard III, who killed two young princes to ensure that he remained King.

Willie, Willie, Harry, Steve
Harry, Dick, John, Harry Three.
Edward One, Two, Three, Dick Two
Henry Four, Five, Six then who?
Edward Four Five, Dick the Bad
Harrys twain and Ned, the lad.
Mary, Lizzie, James the Vain
Charlie, Charlie, James again.
William and Mary, Anne o'Gloria,
Four Georges, William and Victoria
Edward Seven, Georgie Five,
Edward, George and Liz (alive).

Anthem for Doomed Youth

WILFRED OWEN
1893–1918

What passing-bells for these who die as cattle?
   – Only the monstrous anger of the guns.
   Only the stuttering rifles' rapid rattle
Can patter out their hasty orisons.
No mockeries now for them; no prayers nor bells;
   Nor any voice of mourning save the choirs, –
The shrill, demented choirs of wailing shells;
   And bugles calling for them from sad shires.

What candles may be held to speed them all?
   Not in the hands of boys but in their eyes
Shall shine the holy glimmers of goodbyes.
   The pallor of girls' brows shall be their pall;
Their flowers the tenderness of patient minds,
And each slow dusk a drawing-down of blinds.

Casabianca

FELICIA HEMANS
1793–1835

This poem was inspired by the sinking of the French flagship Orient *during the Battle of the Nile in 1798. According to accounts of the time, the thirteen-year-old son of the French commander of* Orient, *Casabianca, refused to desert his post without a direct order. Felicia Hemans contrasts the valour and innocence of the boy with the burning hulk of the ship and shattered dead. The humorous poet Spike Milligan wrote a parody of the poem, using its well-known opening lines: 'The boy stood on the burning deck/Whence all but he had fled – /The twit!'*

The boy stood on the burning deck,
   Whence all but him had fled;
The flame that lit the battle's wreck
   Shone round him o'er the dead.

Yet beautiful and bright he stood,
   As born to rule the storm;
A creature of heroic blood,
   A proud though childlike form.

The flames roll'd on; he would not go
   Without his father's word;
That father, faint in death below,
   His voice no longer heard.

He call'd aloud, 'Say, Father, say,
   If yet my task be done!'
He knew not that the chieftain lay
   Unconscious of his son.

'Speak, Father!' once again he cried,
    'If I may yet be gone!'
And but the booming shots replied,
    And fast the flames roll'd on.

Upon his brow he felt their breath,
    And in his waving hair,
And looked from that lone post of death
    In still yet brave despair;

And shouted but one more aloud,
    'My father, must I stay?'
While o'er him fast, through sail and shroud
    The wreathing fires made way,

They wrapt the ship in splendour wild,
    They caught the flag on high,
And stream'd above the gallant child,
    Like banners in the sky.

There came a burst of thunder sound;
    The boy, – Oh! where was *he*?
Ask of the winds that far around
    With fragments strewed the sea. –

With shroud and mast, and pennon fair,
    That well had borne their part, –
But the noblest thing which perished there
    Was that young, faithful heart.

Does It Matter?

SIEGFRIED SASSOON
1886–1967

Siegfried Sassoon volunteered to join the army in August 1914, soon after the First World War broke out. His patriotic enthusiasm for the cause of war was gradually eroded by the pain and loss that he saw on the battlefield, and this 1916 poem reflects his disenchantment. Bitter with sarcasm, 'Does It Matter?' considers the prospect of a changed world after the war and the need to rebuild lives in the face of loss, injury, shock and grief.

Does it matter? – losing your legs? . . .
For people will always be kind,
And you need not show that you mind
When others come in after hunting
To gobble their muffins and eggs.

Does it matter? – losing your sight? . . .
There's such splendid work for the blind;
And people will always be kind,
As you sit on the terrace remembering
And turning your face to the light.

Do they matter – those dreams from the pit? . . .
You can drink and forget and be glad,
And people won't say that you're mad;
For they know you've fought for your country,
And no one will worry a bit.

Do Not Go Gentle into That Good Night

DYLAN THOMAS

1914–53

Do not go gentle into that good night,
Old age should burn and rave at close of day;
Rage, rage against the dying of the light.

Though wise men at their end know dark is right,
Because their words had forked no lightning they
Do not go gentle into that good night.

Good men, the last wave by, crying how bright
Their frail deeds might have danced in a green bay,
Rage, rage against the dying of the light.

Wild men who caught and sang the sun in flight,
And learn, too late, they grieved it on its way,
Do not go gentle into that good night.

Grave men, near death, who see with blinding sight
Blind eyes could blaze like meteors and be gay,
Rage, rage against the dying of the light.

And you, my father, there on the sad height,
Curse, bless, me now with your fierce tears, I pray,
Do not go gentle into that good night.
Rage, rage against the dying of the light.

My Boy Jack

RUDYARD KIPLING
1865–1936

This poignant poem describes the agony that many parents suffered during the First World War waiting for news of their sons. Rudyard Kipling wrote it after his son John was killed at the battle of Loos in 1915. Here, the 'tide' refers to the sea, but also suggests the movement of fate and the arrival of news. The poem's melancholy tone is combined with the stoical pride that the father feels, knowing that his son has done his duty with honour and courage.

'Have you news of my boy Jack?'
   Not this tide.
'When d'you think that he'll come back?'
   Not with this wind blowing, and this tide.

'Has anyone else had word of him?'
   Not this tide.
   For what is sunk will hardly swim,
   Not with this wind blowing, and this tide.

'Oh, dear, what comfort can I find!'
   None this tide,
   Nor any tide,
Except he did not shame his kind –
   Not even with that wind blowing, and that tide.

Then hold your head up all the more,
   This tide,
   And every tide;
Because he was the son you bore,
   And gave to that wind blowing and that tide!

The Soldier

RUPERT BROOKE
1887–1915

Towards the end of the First World War, disillusion set in and war poetry began
to reflect the horrors faced by British soldiers. However, this poem was written
at the beginning of the war when feelings were still hopeful and idealistic. It reflected
the patriotic mood of the country and was read by the Dean of St Paul's Cathedral in
London to inspire the troops. Traditionally, the sonnet form was used to convey love,
and this reinforces Rupert Brooke's attitude of devotion towards England, as well as
his admiration for the individual soldiers sacrificing themselves. The lines 'there's some
corner of a foreign field / That is forever England' refer to the many men who would be
lost on battlefields abroad and buried in unmarked graves. Brooke died on the Greek
island of Skyros and so was himself buried in 'a foreign field'.

If I should die, think only this of me:
    That there's some corner of a foreign field
That is forever England. There shall be
    In that rich earth a richer dust concealed;
A dust whom England bore, shaped, made aware,
    Gave, once, her flowers to love, her ways to roam,
A body of England's, breathing English air,
    Washed by the rivers, blest by suns of home.

And think, this heart, all evil shed away,
    A pulse in the eternal mind, no less
        Gives somewhere back the thoughts by England given;
    Her sights and sounds; dreams happy as her day;
And laughter, learnt of friends; and gentleness,
    In hearts at peace, under an English heaven.

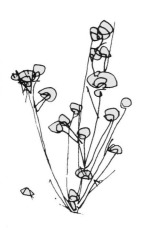

St Crispian's Day

WILLIAM SHAKESPEARE
1564–1616

This soliloquy (a speech, alone on stage) comes from Act 4, Scene 3 of Shakespeare's play Henry V.

This day is call'd the feast of Crispian.
He that outlives this day, and comes safe home,
Will stand a tip-toe when this day is nam'd,
And rouse him at the name of Crispian.
He that shall live this day, and live t'old age,
Will yearly on the vigil feast his neighbours,
And say 'To-morrow is Saint Crispian.'
Then will he strip his sleeve and show his scars,
And say 'These wounds I had on Crispin's day.'
Old men forget; yet all shall be forgot,
But he'll remember, with advantages,
What feats he did that day. Then shall our names,
Familiar in his mouth as household words –
Harry the King, Bedford and Exeter,
Warwick and Talbot, Salisbury and Gloucester –
Be in their flowing cups freshly rememb'red.
This story shall the good man teach his son;
And Crispin Crispian shall ne'er go by,
From this day to the ending of the world,
But we in it shall be rememberéd –
We few, we happy few, we band of brothers;
For he to-day that sheds his blood with me
Shall be my brother; be he ne'er so vile,
This day shall gentle his condition;
And gentlemen in England now a-bed
Shall think themselves accurs'd they were not here,
And hold their manhoods cheap whiles any speaks
That fought with us upon Saint Crispin's day.

Dulce et Decorum Est

WILFRED OWEN
1893–1918

Perhaps the most famous First World War poem, 'Dulce et Decorum Est' describes with brutal realism the soldiers' life in the trenches. The final lines are taken from an ode by the Roman poet Horace and mean 'It is sweet and fitting to die for one's country.' The ode explores the bravery and resourcefulness of the Roman people, but Owen uses the words ironically to suggest that the lives of the young men fighting in the Great War were wasted. Wilfred Owen was killed in action exactly one week before the war ended in 1918.

Bent double, like old beggars under sacks,
Knock-kneed, coughing like hags, we cursed through sludge,
Till on the haunting flares we turned our backs
And toward our distant rest began to trudge.
Men marched asleep. Many had lost their boots
But limped on, blood-shod. All went lame; all blind;
Drunk with fatigue; deaf even to the hoots
Of tired, outstripped Five-Nines that dropped behind.

Gas! GAS! Quick boys! – An ecstasy of fumbling,
Fitting the clumsy helmets just in time;
But something still was yelling and stumbling,
And flound'ring like a man in fire or lime . . .
Dim, through the misty panes and thick green light,
As under a green sea, I saw him drowning.

In all my dreams, before my helpless sight,
He plunges at me, guttering, choking, drowning.
If in some smothering dreams you too could pace
Behind the wagon that we flung him in,

And watch the white eyes writhing in his face,
His hanging face, like a devil's sick of sin;
If you could hear, at every jolt, the blood
Come gargling from the froth-corrupted lungs,
Obscene as cancer, bitter as the cud
Of vile, incurable sores on innocent tongues, –
My friend, you would not tell with such high zest
To children ardent for some desperate glory,
The old Lie: Dulce et decorum est
Pro patria mori.

An Incident of the French Camp

ROBERT BROWNING
1812–89

'An Incident of the French Camp' was inspired by Napoleon's attack on the city of Ratisbon in Bavaria in 1809. The poem is narrated through a speaker who is one of Napoloeon's aides, and uses repetition to emphasize Napoleon's greatness, and the loyalty he inspired in his men. The boy who dies with a smile on his face at the close of this poem was proud to serve such a great man.

You know, we French stormed Ratisbon:
    A mile or so away,
On a little mound, Napoleon
    Stood on our storming-day;
With neck out-thrust, you fancy how,
    Legs wide, arms locked behind,
As if to balance the prone brow
    Oppressive with its mind.

Just as perhaps he mused, 'My plans
    That soar, to earth may fall,
Let once my army-leader Lannes
    Waver at yonder wall,' –
Out 'twixt the battery-smokes there flew
    A rider, bound on bound
Full-galloping; nor bridle drew
    Until he reached the mound.

Then off there flung in smiling joy,
    And held himself erect
By just his horse's mane, a boy:
    You hardly could suspect, –
(So tight he kept his lips compressed
    Scarce any blood came through)

You looked twice ere you saw his breast
    Was all but shot in two.

'Well,' cried he, 'Emperor, by God's grace
    We've got you Ratisbon!
The Marshal's in the market-place,
    And you'll be there anon
To see your flag-bird flap his vans
    Where I, to heart's desire,
Perched him!' The chief's eye flashed; his plans
    Soared up again like fire,

The chief's eye flashed, but presently
    Softened itself, as sheathes
A film the mother-eagle's eye
    When her bruised eaglet breathes,
'You're wounded!' 'Nay,' the soldier's pride
    Touched to the quick, he said:
'I'm killed, Sire!' And his chief beside,
    Smiling the boy fell dead.

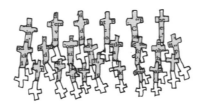

The Charge of the Light Brigade

ALFRED, LORD TENNYSON
1809–92

Tennyson wrote this poem at lightning speed after reading a newspaper article about the devastating 1854 Battle of Balaclava in the Crimean War. Many of the 600 soldiers who charged into battle died as a result of a disastrous miscommunication of orders: 'Someone had blunder'd.' Tennyson's poem reflects the passionate language of the reporter for The Times *as well as a sombre echo from Psalm 23, with its reference to the 'Valley of Death'. There is a sense of grim momentum underlying the poem: Tennyson's use of alliteration and repetition conveys the proud onrush of the cavalry as well as the foolish haste that led to their death.*

Half a league, half a league,
   Half a league onward,
All in the valley of Death
   Rode the six hundred.
'Forward, the Light Brigade!
Charge for the guns!' he said:
Into the valley of Death
   Rode the six hundred.

'Forward, the Light Brigade!'
Was there a man dismay'd?
Not tho' the soldier knew
   Someone had blunder'd:
Their's not to make reply,
Their's not to reason why,
Their's but to do and die:
Into the valley of Death
   Rode the six hundred.

Cannon to right of them,
Cannon to left of them,
Cannon in front of them

Volley'd and thunder'd;
Storm'd at with shot and shell,
Boldly they rode and well,
Into the jaws of Death,
Into the mouth of Hell
    Rode the six hundred.

Flash'd all their sabres bare,
Flash'd as they turn'd in air
Sabring the gunners there,
Charging an army, while
    All the world wonder'd:
Plunged in the battery-smoke
Right thro' the line they broke;
Cossack and Russian
Reel'd from the sabre-stroke
    Shatter'd and sunder'd.
Then they rode back, but not
    Not the six hundred.

Cannon to right of them,
Cannon to left of them,
Cannon behind them
    Volley'd and thunder'd;
Storm'd at with shot and shell,
While horse and hero fell,
They that had fought so well
Came thro' the jaws of Death,
Back from the mouth of Hell,
All that was left of them,
    Left of six hundred.

When can their glory fade?
O the wild charge they made!
    All the world wonder'd.
Honour the charge they made!
Honour the Light Brigade,
    Noble six hundred!

The Battle of Blenheim

ROBERT SOUTHEY
1774–1843

Robert Southey's poem recalls the Battle of Blenheim, which took place in 1704. The Duke of Marlborough used cunning tactics to ambush the Franco-Bavarian army in Vienna, seriously reducing Louis XIV's army, which lost 30,000 soldiers. ''Twas a famous victory' is repeated ironically throughout the poem: nobody really knows why the battle was fought, but it doesn't matter, because the English were victorious. Southey later changed his mind about the battle, stating in 1820 that it was one of the greatest moments in English military history. The Duke of Marlborough was rewarded with a 16,000-acre estate and money to build the very grand Blenheim Palace, where his descendants (one of whom was Sir Winston Churchill) reside to this day.

It was a summer evening,
    Old Kaspar's work was done,
And he before his cottage door
    Was sitting in the sun,
And by him sported on the green
His little grandchild Wilhelmine.

She saw her brother Peterkin
    Roll something large and round,
Which he beside the rivulet
    In playing there had found;
He came to ask what he had found,
That was so large, and smooth, and round.

Old Kaspar took it from the boy,
    Who stood expectant by;
And then the old man shook his head
    And with a natural sigh,
''Tis some poor fellow's skull,' said he,
'Who fell in the great victory.

'I find them in the garden,
    For there's many here about;
And often when I go to plough,
    The ploughshare turns them out!
For many thousand men,' said he,
'Were slain in that great victory.'

'Now tell us what 'twas all about,'
    Young Peterkin, he cries;
And little Wilhelmine looks up
    With wonder-waiting eyes;
'Now tell us all about the war,
And what they fought each other for.'

'It was the English,' Kaspar cried,
    'Who put the French to rout;
But what they fought each other for,
    I could not well make out;
But everybody said,' quoth he,
'That 'twas a famous victory.'

'My father lived at Blenheim then,
    Yon little stream hard by;
They burnt his dwelling to the ground,
    And he was forced to fly;
So with his wife and child he fled,
Nor had he where to rest his head.

'With fire and sword the country round
    Was wasted far and wide,
And many a childing mother then,
    And new-born baby died;
But things like that, you know, must be
At every famous victory.

'They said it was a shocking sight
    After the field was won;
For many thousand bodies here
    Lay rotting in the sun;
But things like that, you know, must be
After a famous victory.

'Great praise the Duke of Marlbro' won,
    And our good Prince Eugene.'
'Why, 'twas a very wicked thing!'
    Said little Wilhelmine.
'Nay . . . nay . . . my little girl,' quoth he,
'It was a famous victory.'

'And everybody praised the Duke
    Who this great fight did win."
'But what good came of it at last?'
    Quoth little Peterkin.
'Why, that I cannot tell,' said he,
'But 'twas a famous victory.'

Jerusalem

WILLIAM BLAKE
1757–1827

This poem is thought to comment on the darkness of the Industrial Revolution. Modernisation brought with it the 'dark satanic mills' and poverty of England's industrial towns, in contrast to the New Jerusalem promised in the Bible's Book of Revelation. Sir Hubert Parry composed the music for Blake's 'Jerusalem' in 1916 and the poem is now better known as a hymn. Although British people now associate it with the Last Night of the Proms and moods of optimistic celebration, it is far from a straightforward patriotic song.

And did those feet in ancient time
Walk upon England's mountains green?
And was the holy Lamb of God
On England's pleasant pastures seen?

And did the countenance divine
Shine forth upon our clouded hills?
And was Jerusalem builded here
Among these dark satanic mills?

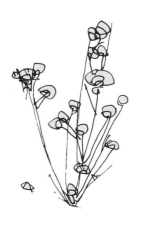

Bring me my bow of burning gold!
Bring me my arrows of desire!
Bring me my spear! O clouds, unfold!
Bring me my chariot of fire!

I will not cease from mental fight,
Nor shall my sword sleep in my hand,
Till we have built Jerusalem
In England's green and pleasant land.

O Captain! My Captain!

WALT WHITMAN

1819–92

This poem is a lament for American President Abraham Lincoln, who was assassinated while at the theatre in 1865. The 'ship' represents America, which had just weathered the storm of a bloody civil war.

O Captain! my Captain! Our fearful trip is done,
The ship has weather'd every rack, the prize we sought is won;
The port is near, the bells I hear, the people all exulting,
While follow eyes the steady keel, the vessel grim and daring;
    But O heart! heart! heart!
      O the bleeding drops of red,
        Where on the deck my Captain lies,
          Fallen cold and dead.

O Captain! my Captain! Rise up and hear the bells;
Rise up – for you the flag is flung – for you the bugle trills,
For you bouquets and ribbon'd wreaths – for you the shores a-crowding;
For you they call, the swaying mass, their eager faces turning;
    Here Captain! dear father!
      This arm beneath your head!
        It is some dream that on the deck,
          You've fallen cold and dead.

My Captain does not answer, his lips are pale and still;
My father does not feel my arm, he has no pulse nor will;
The ship is anchor'd safe and sound, its voyage closed and done;
From fearful trip, the victor ship, comes in with object won;
    Exult O shores, and ring O bells!
      But I with mournful tread,
        Walk the deck my Captain lies,
          Fallen cold and dead.

Old Ironsides

OLIVER WENDELL HOLMES
1809–94

'Old Ironsides' was the nickname given to the US navy ship USS Constitution, first launched in 1797. It earned its nickname after a battle with the British ship HMS Guerriere in 1812. Oliver Wendell Holmes wrote this poem in 1830 in protest over attempts to have Constitution decommissioned. She was a vessel that was hugely popular with the American people, and public opinion saved her from 'the mighty deep'. The USS Constitution now serves as a naval museum in Boston, USA.

Ay, tear her tattered ensign down!
　　Long has it waved on high,
And many an eye has danced to see
　　That banner in the sky;
Beneath it rung the battle shout,
　　And burst the cannon's roar;
The meteor of the ocean air
　　Shall sweep the clouds no more.

Her deck, once red with heroes' blood,
　　Where knelt the vanquished foe,
When winds were hurrying o'er the flood,
　　And waves were white below,
No more shall feel the victor's tread,
　　Or know the conquered knee:
The harpies of the shore shall pluck
　　The eagle of the sea!

Oh, better that her shattered hulk
　　Should sink beneath the wave;
Her thunders shook the mighty deep,
　　And there should be her grave:
Nail to the mast her holy flag,
　　Set every threadbare sail,
And give her to the god of storms,
　　The lightning and the gale!

The Eve of Waterloo

GEORGE GORDON, LORD BYRON
1788–1824

'The Eve of Waterloo' describes a ball held in Brussels three days before the battle of Waterloo of 18 June 1815. There was a seventy-two-hour gap between the ball and the battle, but Byron telescopes this timeframe to increase the dramatic tension. These verses are part of a long narrative poem, 'Childe Harold's Pilgrimage', which is about Byron's world-weary wanderings around Europe and his reflections upon the societies of his time. The battle ended with the English army defeating the French under Napoleon.

There was a sound of revelry by night,
And Belgium's capital had gathered then
Her Beauty and her Chivalry, and bright
The lamps shone o'er fair women and brave men;
A thousand hearts beat happily; and when
Music arose with its voluptuous swell,
Soft eyes looked love to eyes which spake again,
And all went merry as a marriage bell;
But hush! hark! a deep sound strikes like a rising knell!

Did ye not hear it? – No; 'twas but the wind,
Or the car rattling o'er the stony street;
On with the dance! let joy be unconfined;
No sleep till morn, when Youth and Pleasure meet
To chase the glowing Hours with flying feet –
But hark! – that heavy sound breaks in once more,
As if the clouds its echo would repeat;
And nearer, clearer, deadlier than before!
Arm! arm! it is – it is – the cannon's opening roar!

Within a windowed niche of that high hall
Sate Brunswick's fated chieftain; he did hear
That sound the first amidst the festival,
And caught its tone with death's prophetic ear;
And when they smiled because he deemed it near,
His heart more truly knew that peal too well
Which stretched his father on a bloody bier,
And roused the vengeance blood alone could quell;
He rushed into the field, and, foremost fighting, fell.

Ah! then and there was hurrying to and fro,
And gathering tears, and tremblings of distress,
And cheeks all pale, which, but an hour ago,
Blushed at the praise of their own loveliness.
And there were sudden partings, such as press
The life from out young hearts, and choking sighs
Which ne'er might be repeated; who would guess
If ever more should meet those mutual eyes,
Since upon night so sweet such awful morn could rise!

And there was mounting in hot haste; the steed,
The mustering squadron, and the clattering car,
Went pouring forward with impetuous speed,
And swiftly forming in the ranks of war;
And the deep thunder, peal on peal afar;
And near, the beat of the alarming drum
Roused up the soldier ere the morning star;
While thronged the citizens with terror dumb,
Or whispering, with white lips – 'The foe! they come! they come!'

The Star-Spangled Banner

FRANCIS SCOTT KEY
1779–1843

Best known as the American national anthem, 'The Star-Spangled Banner' comes from a poem called 'Defence of Fort McHenry', written in 1814. Francis Scott Key was a lawyer who witnessed the attack on Fort McHenry in Baltimore by the British navy in 1812. It proved to be an American victory over the British, and Key was inspired by the sight of the flag that flew above the fort for the duration of the battle. The English composer John Stafford Smith later set the poem to music. Popular on both sides of the Atlantic, 'The Star-Spangled Banner' became the official flag-raising song for the U.S. Navy in 1889 and was made the national anthem by President Hoover in 1931. The original 'Star-Spangled Banner' flag had thirteen stripes and thirteen stars. Over time, as more states were added, the flag changed. The thirteen stripes remain – they stand for the original colonies – but there are now fifty stars, which each represent one of the Union States.

Oh, say, can you see, by the dawn's early light,
    What so proudly we hailed at the twilight's last gleaming,
Whose broad stripes and bright stars through the perilous fight,
    O'er the ramparts we watched were so gallantly streaming?
And the rockets' red glare, the bombs bursting in air,
Gave proof through the night that our flag was still there.
Oh, say does that star-spangled banner yet wave
O'er the land of the free and the home of the brave!

On the shore, dimly seen through the mists of the deep,
    Where the foe's haughty host in dread silence reposes,
What is that which the breeze o'er the towering steep,
    As it fitfully blows, half conceals, half discloses?
Now it catches the gleam of the morning's first beam,
In full glory reflected, now shines in the stream.
'Tis the star-spangled banner; oh, long may it wave
O'er the land of the free, and the home of the brave!

And where is that band who so vauntingly swore
 That the havoc of war and the battle's confusion
A home and a country should leave us no more?
 Their blood has washed out their foul footsteps' pollution.
No refuge could save the hireling and slave
From the terror of flight, or the gloom of the grave:
And the star-spangled banner in triumph doth wave
O'er the land of the free, and the home of the brave!

Oh, thus be it ever, when freemen shall stand
 Between their loved homes and the war's desolation;
Blest with victory and peace, may the heaven-rescued land
 Praise the power that hath made and preserved us a nation!
Then conquer we must, when our cause it is just,
And this be our motto: 'In God is our trust!'
And the star-spangled banner in triumph doth wave
O'er the land of the free, and the home of the brave!

Death Be Not Proud

JOHN DONNE
1572–1631

his is a sonnet addressed to death portrayed as a person, and as such is a fine example of personification. It is written in the sonnet form known as 'Petrarchan', which is named after the Italian poet Francesco Petrarch. The Petrarchan sonnet has fourteen lines; typically, the first eight lines set a problem that is then resolved in the last six. 'Death Be Not Proud' is the tenth in John Donne's series of nineteen Holy Sonnets, which reflect on religious subjects. In the seventeenth century, when John Donne was writing, the Church preached that the wicked would go to hell when they died, terrifying many of its followers. By personifying death, John Donne makes the concept less mysterious and frightening to readers then and now.

Death be not proud, though some have called thee
Mighty and dreadfull, for, thou art not soe,
For, those, whom thou think'st, thou dost overthrow,
Die not, poore death, nor yet canst thou kill mee;
From rest and sleepe, which but thy pictures bee,
Much pleasure, then from thee, much more must flow,
And soonest our best men with thee doe goe,
Rest of their bones, and soules deliverie.
Thou art slave to Fate, chance, kings, and desperate men,
And dost with poyson, warre, and sicknesse dwell,
And poppie, or charmes can make us sleepe as well,
And better then thy stroake; why swell'st thou then?
One short sleepe past, wee wake eternally,
And death shall be no more; Death thou shalt die.

Requiescat

MATTHEW ARNOLD
1822–88

'Requiescat' is a Latin word denoting a traditional prayer said for the souls of the dead. It actually means: 'May he/she rest' or 'Rest in peace'. Here death is shown as a release into something fuller, instead of a bleak ending. The yew is a traditional symbol of death, whereas roses represent beauty and love. Perhaps Matthew Arnold is writing about a woman he loved and lost. Whoever she is, she seems to be weary of life and craving the peace of death. The poet's pleas to have roses strewn upon her grave show the extent to which he wishes to celebrate her vitality in life rather than mourn her passing.

Strew on her roses, roses,
    And never a spray of yew!
In quiet she reposes;
    Ah, would that I did too!

Her mirth the world required;
    She bathed it in smiles of glee.
But her heart was tired, tired,
    And now they let her be.

Her life was turning, turning,
    In mazes of heat and sound.
But for peace her soul was yearning,
    And now peace laps her round.

Her cabin'd, ample spirit,
    It flutter'd and fail'd for breath.
Tonight it doth inherit
    The vasty hall of death.

Crossing the Bar

ALFRED, LORD TENNYSON
1809–1892

If you read this poem aloud, you will notice that the rhythm is irregular, perhaps reflecting the waves at sea. Tennyson uses the sea as a metaphor for life, referring to the ultimate voyage towards death as crossing the bar. A sandbar is a ridge of sand and pebbles underwater, which can often mark a change, like the move from a river into the sea. The poem takes place at sunset, reinforcing the idea that Tennyson's narrator is embarking upon a mysterious transition. The 'Pilot' he hopes to see is most probably God, an interpretation supported by the word having a capital 'P'. Just before he died, Tennyson asked to have 'Crossing the Bar' placed at the end of all his poetry anthologies.

Sunset and evening star,
    And one clear call for me!
And may there be no moaning of the bar,
    When I put out to sea,

But such a tide as moving seems asleep,
    Too full for sound and foam,
When that which drew from out the boundless deep
    Turns again home.

Twilight and evening bell,
    And after that the dark!
And may there be no sadness of farewell,
    When I embark;

For tho' from out our bourne of Time and Place
    The flood may bear me far,
I hope to see my Pilot face to face
    When I have crost the bar.

Lessons for Life

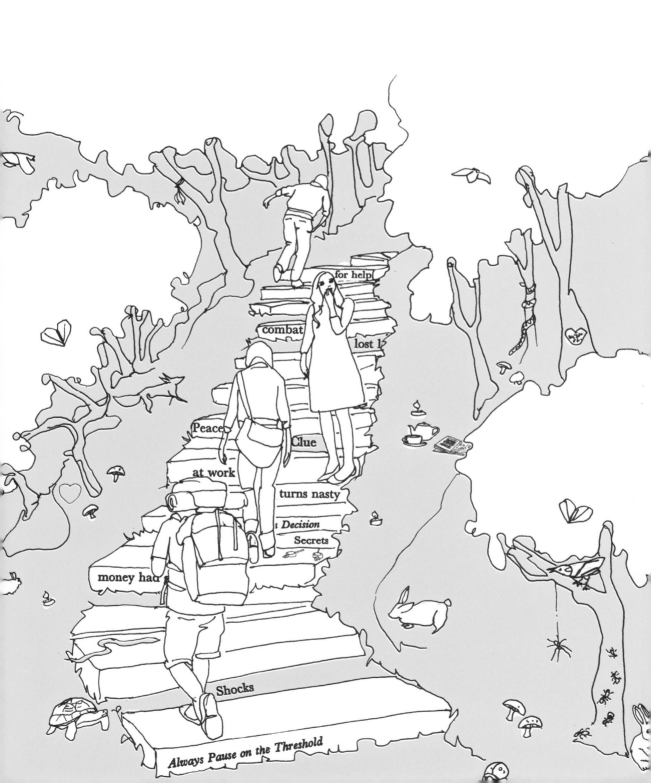

Little Things

EBENEZER COBHAM BREWER
1810–97

An ocean can be divided into 'drops of water' and a beach into 'grains of sand' as a way of understanding their vastness. It is difficult for us to understand 'eternity', but if you imagine each minute, it is easier to comprehend. You can apply the idea to anything that seems too big to think about, such as philosophy or science, or even a huge pile of homework.

Little drops of water,
Little grains of sand,
Make the mighty ocean
And the pleasant land.

Thus the little minutes,
Humble though they be,
Make the mighty ages
Of eternity.

Our Saviour's Golden Rule

ISAAC WATTS
1674–1748

Be you to others kind and true,
As you'd have others be to you;
And neither do nor say to men
Whate'er you would not take again.

The Frog

HILAIRE BELLOC
1870–1953

Be kind and tender to the Frog,
    And do not call him names,
As 'Slimy skin', or 'Polly-wog',
    Or likewise 'Ugly James',
Or 'Gap-a-grin', or 'Toad-gone-wrong',
    Or 'Bill Bandy-knees':
The Frog is justly sensitive
    To epithets like these.
No animal will more repay
    A treatment kind and fair;
At least so lonely people say
Who keep a frog (and, by the way,
They are extremely rare).

The Way through the Woods

RUDYARD KIPLING
1865–1936

This poem uses the road through the woods as a metaphor for the path of someone's life.

They shut the road through the woods
Seventy years ago.
Weather and rain have undone it again,
And now you would never know
There was once a road through the woods
Before they planted the trees.
It is underneath the coppice and heath
And the thin anemones.
Only the keeper sees
That, where the ring-dove broods,
And the badgers roll at ease,
There was once a road through the woods.

Yet, if you enter the woods
Of a summer evening late,
When the night-air cools on the trout-ringed pools
Where the otter whistles his mate,
(They fear not men in the woods,
Because they see so few.)
You will hear the beat of a horse's feet,
And the swish of a skirt in the dew,
Steadily cantering through
The misty solitudes,
As though they perfectly knew
The old lost road through the woods . . .
But there is no road through the woods.

Timothy Winters

CHARLES CAUSLEY
1917–2003

Timothy Winters comes to school
With eyes as wide as a football pool,
Ears like bombs and teeth like splinters:
A blitz of a boy is Timothy Winters.

His belly is white, his neck is dark,
And his hair is an exclamation mark.
His clothes are enough to scare a crow
And through his britches the blue winds blow.

When teacher talks he won't hear a word
And he shoots down dead the arithmetic-bird,
He licks the pattern off his plate
And he's not even heard of the Welfare State.

Timothy Winters has bloody feet
And he lives in a house on Suez Street,
He sleeps in a sack on the kitchen floor
And they say there aren't boys like him anymore.

Old Man Winters likes his beer
And his missus ran off with a bombardier,
Grandma sits in the grate with a gin
And Timothy's dosed with an aspirin.

The Welfare Worker lies awake
But the law's as tricky as a ten-foot snake,
So Timothy Winters drinks his cup
And slowly goes on growing up.

At Morning Prayers the Master helves
For children less fortunate than ourselves,
And the loudest response in the room is when
Timothy Winters roars 'Amen!'

So come one angel, come on ten:
Timothy Winters says 'Amen
Amen amen amen amen.'
Timothy Winters, Lord.

                              Amen.

'Hope' is the Thing with Feathers

EMILY DICKINSON
1830–86

This poem uses metaphor to define hope by comparing it to a bird. It is difficult to imagine a small and delicate bird being able to fly long distances or live through a storm, but the bird's tuneful singing reminds us that hope is always there, even if hidden.

'Hope' is the thing with feathers –
That perches in the soul –
And sings the tune without the words –
And never stops – at all –

And sweetest – in the Gale – is heard –
And sore must be the storm –
That could abash the little Bird
That kept so many warm –

I've heard it in the chillest land –
And on the strangest Sea –
Yet – never – in Extremity,
It asked a crumb – of me.

If

RUDYARD KIPLING
1865–1936

This poem about stoicism invites the reader to think about the kind of person they aspire to be. Rudyard Kipling wrote in his autobiography that he was inspired to write 'If' by the bravery of the Scottish colonial leader Dr Leander Starr Jameson against the Boers in South Africa. Rudyard Kipling was famous for writing patriotic verse, and this poem reflects a desire to instil bravery and virtue in the future defenders of the British Empire. The lines 'If you can meet with Triumph and Disaster and treat those two impostors just the same' are written above the players' entrance to the Centre Court at Wimbledon.

If you can keep your head when all about you
 Are losing theirs and blaming it on you,
If you can trust yourself when all men doubt you,
 But make allowance for their doubting too;
If you can wait and not be tired by waiting,
 Or being lied about, don't deal in lies,
Or being hated, don't give way to hating,
 And yet don't look too good, nor talk too wise:

If you can dream – and not make dreams your master;
 If you can think – and not make thoughts your aim;
If you can meet with Triumph and Disaster
 And treat those two impostors just the same;
If you can bear to hear the truth you've spoken
 Twisted by knaves to make a trap for fools,
Or watch the things you gave your life to, broken,
 And stoop and build 'em up with worn-out tools:

If you can make one heap of all your winnings
    And risk it on one turn of pitch-and-toss,
And lose, and start again at your beginnings
    And never breathe a word about your loss;
If you can force your heart and nerve and sinew
    To serve your turn long after they are gone,
And so hold on when there is nothing in you
    Except the Will which says to them: 'Hold on!'

If you can talk with crowds and keep your virtue,
    Or walk with Kings – nor lose the common touch,
If neither foes nor loving friends can hurt you,
    If all men count with you, but none too much;
If you can fill the unforgiving minute
    With sixty seconds' worth of distance run,
Yours is the Earth and everything that's in it,
    And – which is more – you'll be a Man, my son!

A Farewell

CHARLES KINGSLEY
1819–75

My fairest child, I have no song to give you;
    No lark could pipe to skies so dull and grey:
Yet, ere we part, one lesson I can leave you
    For every day.

Be good, sweet maid, and let who will be clever;
    Do noble things, not dream them, all day long:
And so make life, death, and that vast for-ever
    One grand, sweet song.

Musée des Beaux Arts

W. H. AUDEN
1907–73

W. H. Auden refers to a painting called 'Icarus', which hangs in the Musées Royaux des Beaux Arts de Belgique in Brussels. Icarus is a tragic figure from Greek mythology who flew too close to the sun and the wax that held his wings together melted, causing him to plunge into the sea. The painting by Brueghel shows Icarus drowning, unnoticed, in the corner of the canvas. In his poem, Auden emphasizes how suffering and tragedy are an inseparable part of everyday life.

About suffering they were never wrong,
The Old Masters: how well they understood
Its human position; how it takes place
While someone else is eating or opening a window or just walking dully along;
How, when the aged are reverently, passionately waiting
For the miraculous birth, there always must be
Children who did not specially want it to happen, skating
On a pond at the edge of the wood:
They never forgot
That even the dreadful martyrdom must run its course
Anyhow in a corner, some untidy spot
Where the dogs go on with their doggy life and the torturer's horse
Scratches its innocent behind on a tree.

In Brueghel's *Icarus*, for instance: how everything turns away
Quite leisurely from the disaster; the ploughman may
Have heard the splash, the forsaken cry,
But for him it was not an important failure; the sun shone
As it had to on the white legs disappearing into the green
Water; and the expensive delicate ship that must have seen
Something amazing, a boy falling out of the sky,
Had somewhere to get to and sailed calmly on.

Up-hill

CHRISTINA ROSSETTI
1830–94

Christina Rossetti filled her poems with religious imagery. This poem is a simple example of an allegory, a poetic technique which tells two stories at the same time. In 'Up-hill', we know that the conversation is about heaven, the 'inn' where people can rest after their life's long journey. The question and answer format creates questions itself. Who is speaking? Who is replying? It could be an old man seeking reassurance from God, a child trying to understand death, or any number of other possibilities. This gives the poem its charm and accessibility; we can imagine anyone, including ourselves, thinking of these questions and seeking answers.

Does the road wind up-hill all the way?
    Yes, to the very end.
Will the day's journey take the whole long day?
    From morn to night, my friend.

But is there for the night a resting-place?
    A roof for when the slow dark hours begin.
May not the darkness hide it from my face?
    You cannot miss that inn.

Shall I meet other wayfarers at night?
    Those who have gone before.
Then must I knock, or call when just in sight?
    They will not keep you standing at that door.

Shall I find comfort, travel-sore and weak?
    Of labour you shall find the sum.
Will there be beds for me and all who seek?
    Yea, beds for all who come.

Invictus

W. E. HENLEY
1849–1903

It is thought that W.E. Henley was inspired to write this poem after his foot was amputated, having suffered tuberculosis. 'Invictus' (the Latin for 'unconquered') is a poem that breathes defiance and courage. The personification of 'chance' and 'circumstance' allow us to picture the poet's struggles against these figures, and the simplicity of the poem's structure allows the powerful words to speak for themselves. Nelson Mandela is said to have read 'Invictus' to his fellow prisoners while incarcerated on Robben Island.

Out of the night that covers me,
    Black as the Pit from pole to pole,
I thank whatever gods may be
    For my unconquerable soul.

In the fell clutch of circumstance
    I have not winced nor cried aloud.
Under the bludgeonings of chance
    My head is bloody, but unbowed.

Beyond this place of wrath and tears
    Looms but the Horror of the shade,
And yet the menace of the years
    Finds, and shall find, me unafraid.

It matters not how strait the gate,
    How charged with punishments the scroll,
I am the master of my fate:
    I am the captain of my soul.

Say Not the Struggle Naught Availeth

ARTHUR HUGH CLOUGH
1819–61

This inspirational poem was quoted by Winston Churchill in one of his famous wartime speeches. Arthur Hugh Clough is encouraging us to persevere, and assures us that we will then emerge stronger from the conflict.

Say not the struggle naught availeth,
　　The labour and the wounds are vain,
The enemy faints not, nor faileth,
　　And as things have been they remain.

If hopes were dupes, fears may be liars;
　　It may be, in yon smoke concealed,
Your comrades chase e'en now the fliers,
　　And, but for you, possess the field.

For while the tired waves, vainly breaking,
　　Seem here no painful inch to gain,
Far back, through creeks and inlets making,
　　Comes silent, flooding in, the main.

And not by eastern windows only,
　　When daylight comes, comes in the light;
In front the sun climbs slow, how slowly,
　　But westward, look, the land is bright!

The Road Not Taken

ROBERT FROST
1874–1963

Two roads diverged in a yellow wood,
And sorry I could not travel both
And be one traveler, long I stood
And looked down one as far as I could
To where it bent in the undergrowth;

Then took the other, as just as fair,
And having perhaps the better claim,
Because it was grassy and wanted wear;
Though as for that, the passing there
Had worn them really about the same,

And both that morning equally lay
In leaves no step had trodden black.
Oh, I kept the first for another day!
Yet knowing how way leads on to way,
I doubted if I should ever come back.

I shall be telling this with a sigh
Somewhere ages and ages hence:
Two roads diverged in a wood, and I –
I took the one less traveled by,
And that has made all the difference.

Ozymandias

PERCY BYSSHE SHELLEY
1792–1822

*P*ercy Bysshe Shelley had a sonnet competition with his friend and colleague Horace Smith; they composed poems on the same subject and submitted them to the literary magazine The Examiner. Shelley wrote 'Ozymandias', while Horace Smith gave his effort the rather eccentric title 'On a Stupendous Leg of Granite, Discovered Standing by Itself in the Deserts of Egypt, with the Inscription Inserted Below'! Their subject was the Egyptian pharaoh Rameses II, who had a statue of himself made bearing the self-aggrandising inscription 'King of Kings am I, Ozymandias'. Shelley mocks this arrogance, describing a colossus in ruins. Both friends had their poems published in the magazine.

I met a traveller from an antique land
Who said: 'Two vast and trunkless legs of stone
Stand in the desert. Near them on the sand,
Half sunk, a shatter'd visage lies, whose frown
And wrinkled lip and sneer of cold command
Tell that its sculptor well those passions read
Which yet survive, stamp'd on these lifeless things,
The hand that mock'd them and the heart that fed;
And on the pedestal these words appear:
'My name is Ozymandias, king of kings:
Look on my works, ye Mighty, and despair!'
Nothing beside remains. Round the decay
Of that colossal wreck, boundless and bare,
The lone and level sands stretch far away.

One Art

ELIZABETH BISHOP
1911–79

'One Art' is a striking example of the 'villanelle', a complex poetic form based on a strict pattern of rhyme and repetition. In this poem, Bishop uses this rigid structure to regulate the experience of loss and, simultaneously, control grief. The main rhyming words – 'master' and 'disaster' – are locked into carefully crafted dialogue. As the poem develops, the images of 'lost things' grow in size and significance: we move from 'lost door keys' to lost 'houses', and even a lost 'continent'. The final quatrain – suddenly introducing the 'you' pronoun – addresses a very personal, very human loss. The enormity of this final loss is almost enough to disrupt poetic form, but the speaker forces herself to '(Write it!)' and complete the concluding rhyme of the villanelle. In this sense, the poem is like a performance: it both describes, and makes, an 'art of losing'.

The art of losing isn't hard to master;
so many things seem filled with the intent
to be lost that their loss is no disaster.

Lose something every day. Accept the fluster
of lost door keys, the hour badly spent.
The art of losing isn't hard to master.

Then practice losing farther, losing faster:
places, and names, and where it was you meant
to travel. None of these will bring disaster.

I lost my mother's watch. And look! my last, or
next-to-last, of three loved houses went.
The art of losing isn't hard to master.

I lost two cities, lovely ones. And, vaster,
some realms I owned, two rivers, a continent.
I miss them, but it wasn't a disaster.

– Even losing you (the joking voice, a gesture
I love) I shan't have lied. It's evident
the art of losing's not too hard to master
though it may look like (*Write* it!) like disaster.

Humility

ROBERT HERRICK
1591–1674

As one of the central messages of the Christian faith, the virtue of humility is something that would have been important to Robert Herrick, who was a clergyman. This simple poem reflects the sentiments of the New Testament, which tells us that 'the humble shall be honoured'. Each line of the poem is broken by a caesura, a deliberate pause that strengthens the rhythm of the poem. It is a good way of making the reader really think about the sentiments of the verse.

Humble we must be, if to Heaven we go:
High is the roof there; but the gate is low.
Whene'er thou speak'st, look with a lowly eye:
Grace is increased by humility.

Caged Bird

MAYA ANGELOU
1928–

The caged bird symbolizes the oppression that African Americans endured as a result of the legacy of slavery. The language is stark and the poem's structure is similarly plain. Just as the struggle lay in an unjust contrast between black and white, so the poem contrasts images of freedom and captivity.

The free bird leaps
on the back of the wind
and floats downstream
till the current ends
and dips his wing
in the orange sun rays
and dares to claim the sky.

But a bird that stalks
down his narrow cage
can seldom see through
his bars of rage
his wings are clipped and
his feet are tied
so he opens his throat to sing.

The caged bird sings
with a fearful trill
of things unknown
but longed for still
and his tune is heard
on the distant hill
for the caged bird
sings of freedom.

The free bird thinks of another breeze
and the trade winds soft through the sighing trees
and the fat worms waiting on a dawn-bright lawn
and he names the sky his own.

But a caged bird stands on the grave of dreams
his shadow shouts on a nightmare scream
his wings are clipped and his feet are tied
so he opens his throat to sing.

The caged bird sings
with a fearful trill
of things unknown
but longed for still
and his tune is heard
on the distant hill
for the caged bird
sings of freedom.

Not Waving but Drowning

STEVIE SMITH

1902–71

The poem's title and refrain have entered the English language as an expression for someone who is struggling while onlookers think he or she is just larking about. It could be read as a poem about a man dying or as a metaphor for the feeling of spiritual death he is feeling at being misunderstood. 'Not Waving but Drowning' is often read as an analysis of Stevie Smith's own troubles, and as such is an example of an 'autobiographical' poem – a poem which reflects the poet's own life.

Nobody heard him, the dead man,
But still he lay moaning:
I was much further out than you thought
And not waving but drowning.

Poor chap, he always loved larking
And now he's dead.
It must have been too cold for him his heart gave way,
They said.

Oh, no no no, it was too cold always
(Still the dead one lay moaning)
I was much too far out all my life
And not waving but drowning.

Bedtime

Hush Little Baby

ANON

The rhyme in each line of this poem makes it easy to remember, and might explain some of the odd rewards being offered by a mother to get her child to sleep!

Hush, little baby, don't say a word,
Mama's gonna buy you a mockingbird.
If that mockingbird don't sing,
Mama's gonna buy you a diamond ring.
If that diamond ring gets broke,
Mama's gonna buy you a billy goat.
If that billy goat won't pull,
Mama's gonna buy you a cart and bull.
If that cart and bull turn over,
Mama's gonna buy you a dog named Rover.
If that dog named Rover won't bark.
Mama's gonna buy you a horse and cart.
If that horse and cart fall down,
You'll still be the sweetest little baby in town.
So hush little baby, don't you cry,
'Cause Daddy loves you and so do I.

The Land of Nod

ROBERT LOUIS STEVENSON
1850–94

From breakfast on through all the day
At home among my friends I stay;
But every night I go abroad
Afar into the land of Nod.

All by myself I have to go,
With none to tell me what to do –
All alone beside the streams
And up the mountain-sides of dreams.

The strangest things are there for me,
Both things to eat and things to see,
And many frightening sights abroad
Till morning in the land of Nod.

Try as I like to find the way,
I never can get back by day,
Nor can remember plain and clear
The curious music that I hear.

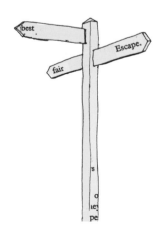

The Star

JANE TAYLOR
1783–1824

This poem first appeared in Rhymes for the Nursery, *published in 1806 by sisters Ann and Jane Taylor. The first verse is one of our best-known nursery rhymes, while the later lines are almost completely forgotten. The sing-song words and repetition make it easy to learn .*

Twinkle, twinkle, little star,
How I wonder what you are!
Up above the world so high,
Like a diamond in the sky.

When the blazing sun is gone,
When he nothing shines upon,
Then you show your little light,
Twinkle, twinkle, all the night.

Then the traveller in the dark,
Thanks you for your tiny spark,
He could not see which way to go,
If you did not twinkle so.

In the dark blue sky you keep,
And often through my curtains peep,
For you never shut your eye,
Till the sun is in the sky.

As your bright and tiny spark,
Lights the traveller in the dark,
Though I know now what you are,
Twinkle, twinkle, little star.

Bed in Summer

ROBERT LOUIS STEVENSON
1850–94

In winter I get up at night
And dress by yellow candle-light.
In summer, quite the other way,
I have to go to bed by day.

I have to go to bed and see
The birds still hopping on the tree,
Or hear the grown-up people's feet
Still going past me in the street.

And does it not seem hard to you,
When all the sky is clear and blue,
And I should like so much to play,
To have to go to bed by day?

Wynken, Blynken, and Nod

EUGENE FIELD
1850–95

This poem, written by the American poet and journalist Eugene Field, is also known as 'Dutch Lullaby'. It lulls us gently into dreamland. Do you ever find that just before you go to sleep, your imagination can run wild and dreams seem real? What poem would you write to describe your dreams?

Wynken, Blynken, and Nod one night
    Sailed off in a wooden shoe –
Sailed on a river of crystal light,
    Into a sea of dew.
'Where are you going, and what do you wish?'
    The old moon asked the three.
'We have come to fish for the herring fish
    That live in this beautiful sea;
    Nets of silver and gold have we!'
      Said Wynken,
      Blynken,
      And Nod.

The old moon laughed and sang a song,
    As they rocked in the wooden shoe,
And the wind that sped them all night long
    Ruffled the waves of dew.
The little stars were the herring fish
    That lived in that beautiful sea –
'Now cast your nets wherever you wish –
    Never afeard are we';
    So cried the stars to the fishermen three:
      Wynken,
      Blynken,
      And Nod.

All night long their nets they threw
　　To the stars in the twinkling foam –
Then down from the skies came the wooden shoe,
　　Bringing the fishermen home;
'Twas all so pretty a sail it seemed
　　As if it could not be,
And some folks thought 'twas a dream they'd dreamed
　　Of sailing that beautiful sea –
　　But I shall name you the fishermen three:
　　　　Wynken,
　　　　Blynken,
　　　　And Nod.

Wynken and Blynken are two little eyes,
　　And Nod is a little head,
And the wooden shoe that sailed the skies
　　Is a wee one's trundle-bed.
So shut your eyes while mother sings
　　Of wonderful sights that be,
And you shall see the beautiful things
　　As you rock in the misty sea,
　　Where the old shoe rocked the fishermen three:
　　　　Wynken,
　　　　Blynken,
　　　　And Nod.

The Race to Get to Sleep

BRIAN PATTEN
1946–

They're on their marks, they're set,
They're off!

Matthew's kicking off his shoes!
Penny's struggling out of her jumper!
He's ripping off his trousers!
She's got one sock off! Now the other's off!
But Matthew's still winning! No, he's not!
It's Penny! Penny's in the lead!
She's down to her knickers!
She's racing out of the room!
She's racing upstairs!
Matthew's right behind her!
There's a fight on the landing!
There's a scramble at the bathroom door!
It's Penny! It's Matthew! It's…
Splash! They're both in the bath!
But there's a hitch!
Matthew's got soap in his eye!
Penny's got soap up her nose!
They're stalling! But no, they're both fine!
They're both out of the bath! They're neck and neck!
It's Matthew! It's Penny! It's Matthew!
Now it's Penny again! She's ahead!
She's first on with her pyjamas!
Now Matthew's catching up! There's nothing in it!
They're climbing into their beds!
Matthew's in the lead with one eye closed!
Now it's Penny again! She's got both closed!
So's Matthew! He's catching up!
It's impossible to tell who's winning!

They're both absolutely quiet!
There's not a murmur from either of them.
It's Matthew! It's Penny! It's …
It's a draw! A draw!
But no! Wait a moment! It's not a draw!
Matthew's opened an eye!
He's asking if Penny's asleep yet!
He's disqualified!
So's Penny! She's doing the same!
She's asking if Matthew's asleep yet!
It's impossible! It's daft!
It's the hardest race in the whole world!

A Child's Evening Prayer

SAMUEL TAYLOR COLERIDGE
1772–1834

Ere on my bed my limbs I lay,
God grant me grace my prayers to say:
O God! preserve my mother dear
In strength and health for many a year;
And, O! preserve my father too,
And may I pay him reverence due;
And may I my best thoughts employ
To be my parents' hope and joy;
And, O! preserve my brothers both
From evil doings and from sloth,
And may we always love each other
Our friends, our father, and our mother:
And still, O Lord, to me impart
An innocent and grateful heart,
That after my great sleep I may
Awake to thy eternal day!

Amen.

The Land of Counterpane

ROBERT LOUIS STEVENSON
1850–94

As a child growing up in Edinburgh, Robert Louis Stevenson was often unwell and forced to stay in bed. To keep boredom at bay, he would make up stories and poems, his imagination fired by reading his favourite book, The Arabian Nights. 'The Land of Counterpane' imagines the secret life of a child just like Stevenson, stuck in bed. The bedclothes are transformed into hills through which his soldiers travel, the sheets into seas ready for his ships, while he himself becomes the giant sitting on the 'pillow-hill' in the pleasant land he has created. We all have secret worlds and Stevenson has magically shared his: what would your secret world look like?

When I was sick and lay a-bed,
I had two pillows at my head,
And all my toys beside me lay
To keep me happy all the day.

And sometimes for an hour or so
I watched my leaden soldiers go,
With different uniforms and drills,
Among the bed-clothes, through the hills;

And sometimes sent my ships in fleets
All up and down among the sheets;
Or brought my trees and houses out,
And planted cities all about.

I was the giant great and still
That sits upon the pillow-hill,
And sees before him, dale and plain,
The pleasant land of counterpane.

The Crescent Moon

AMY LOWELL
1874–1925

Slipping softly through the sky
    Little horned, happy moon,
Can you hear me up so high?
    Will you come down soon?

On my nursery window-sill
    Will you stay your steady flight?
And then float away with me
    Through the summer night?

Brushing over tops of trees,
    Playing hide and seek with stars,
Peeping up through shiny clouds
    At Jupiter or Mars.

I shall fill my lap with roses
    Gathered in the milky way,
All to carry home to mother.
    Oh! what will she say!

Little rocking, sailing moon,
Do you hear me shout – Ahoy!
Just a little nearer, moon,
    To please a little boy.

Escape at Bedtime

ROBERT LOUIS STEVENSON
1850–94

In another of his poems about bedtime, Robert Louis Stevenson captures a child's sense of wonder as he escapes outside to look at the vast sky.

The lights from the parlour and kitchen shone out
    Through the blinds and the windows and bars;
And high overhead and all moving about,
    There were thousands of millions of stars.
There ne'er were such thousands of leaves on a tree,
    Nor of people in church or the Park,
As the crowds of the stars that looked down upon me,
    And that glittered and winked in the dark.

The Dog, and the Plough, and the Hunter, and all,
    And the star of the sailor, and Mars,
These shown in the sky, and the pail by the wall
    Would be half full of water and stars.
They saw me at last, and they chased me with cries,
    And they soon had me packed into bed;
But the glory kept shining and bright in my eyes,
    And the stars going round in my head.

Sweet and Low

ALFRED, LORD TENNYSON
1809–92

Sweet and low, sweet and low,
   Wind of the western sea,
Low, low, breathe and blow,
   Wind of the western sea!
Over the rolling waters go,
Come from the dying moon, and blow,
   Blow him again to me;
While my little one, while my pretty one sleeps.

Sleep and rest, sleep and rest,
   Father will come to thee soon;
Rest, rest, on mother's breast,
   Father will come to thee soon;
Father will come to his babe in the nest,
Silver sails all out of the west
   Under the silver moon:
Sleep, my little one, sleep, my pretty one, sleep.

The Night Mail

W.H. AUDEN
1907–73

'The Night Mail' shows how communication crosses all social barriers; everyone whether rich or poor relies on the interest and friendship of others to feel part of a larger community. Every letter carried by the rushing train has a separate and distinct meaning for its recipient. From bills to love-letters, job applications to exchanges of gossip, each letter reassures someone that they are important and their life is significant. The poem cleverly evokes the rhythm of the train's journey through the town and country: the pace of the verse slows down as the train climbs a hill and then as the train speeds up, so the lines quicken too.

This is the night mail crossing the Border,
Bringing the cheque and the postal order,

Letters for the rich, letters for the poor,
The shop at the corner, the girl next door.

Pulling up Beattock, a steady climb:
The gradient's against her, but she's on time.

Past cotton-grass and moorland boulder,
Shovelling white steam over her shoulder,

Snorting noisily as she passes
Silent miles of wind-bent grasses.

Birds turn their heads as she approaches,
Stare from bushes at her blank-faced coaches.

Sheep-dogs cannot turn her course;
They slumber on with paws across.

In the farm she passes no one wakes,
But a jug in a bedroom gently shakes.

Dawn freshens. Her climb is done.
Down towards Glasgow she descends,
Towards the steam tugs yelping down a glade of cranes,
Towards the fields of apparatus, the furnaces
Set on the dark plain like gigantic chessmen.
All Scotland waits for her:
In dark glens, beside pale-green lochs,
Men long for news.

Letters of thanks, letters from banks,
Letters of joy from girl and boy,
Receipted bills and invitations
To inspect new stock or visit relations,
And applications for situations,
And timid lovers' declarations,
And gossip, gossip from all the nations,
News circumstantial, news financial,
Letters with holiday snaps to enlarge in,
Letters with faces scrawled on the margin,
Letters from uncles, cousins and aunts,
Letters to Scotland from the South of France,
Letters of condolence to Highlands and Lowlands,
Written on paper of every hue,
The pink, the violet, the white and the blue,
The chatty, the catty, the boring, adoring,
The cold and official and the heart's outpouring,
Clever, stupid, short and long,
The typed and the printed and the spelt all wrong.

Thousands are still asleep
Dreaming of terrifying monsters
Or a friendly tea beside the band in Cranston's or Crawford's;
Asleep in working Glasgow, asleep in well-set Edinburgh,
Asleep in granite Aberdeen,
They continue their dreams,
But shall wake soon and long for letters,
And none will hear the postman's knock
Without a quickening of the heart,
For who can bear to feel himself forgotten?

Poems For Possibilities

This is our sticking-plaster index. If you are in some sort of trouble, or need to escape, or could do with some wise words to help you through life's hurlyburly, these poems may help.

IF YOU NEED COURAGE ...

If you need lead in your pencil when facing an exam or a dose of courage to play in a sports match with impossible odds, these are the poems to help stiffen your resolve. They could help those facing more serious challenges too.

IF YOU SEEK GUIDANCE ...

There is guidance here for almost every possibility – from Emily Brontë's thoughts on friendship to William Shakespeare's examination of life's different stages. Some advice is humorous; some serious. We named our anthology 'iF' after the Kipling poem, which has advice aplenty.

IF YOU ARE FACING GRIEF …

We hope those facing loss may find some consolation here.

IF YOU NEED A POCKET FULL OF PEACE …

If life for whatever reason is overwhelming, a poem can be a pocket full of peace. Many of these poems evoke the tranquillity of nature. We hope they may lend you a sense of quiet and calm.

Poetic Terms

ALLITERATION

Deliberately using words that begin with the same letter usually, but not always, next to one another; for example, a 'grim, gloomy gushing river'. The effect varies according to the letter used. A soft 'f' or 'l' can create a lush and peaceful atmosphere, while an alliterative 'b' or 'd' is harder and more dramatic. Many cartoon characters have alliterative names to make them more memorable. If Mickey Mouse had been called Ebenezer instead, he might not have been so enormously successful.

RHYME

Moon/June, Love/Dove. You know what this is. Rhyme is often used to create a sense of momentum in the poem and can also create moments of humour. When you are talking about a poem, it is useful to know about rhyme schemes. For instance, the beginning of Shakespeare's Sonnet 18:

> Shall I compare thee to a Summer's day?   *a*
> Thou art more lovely and more temperate: *b*
> Rough winds do shake the darling buds of May,   *a*
> And Summer's lease hath all too short a date: *b*

So each of the pairs of rhymes are identified with *a* or *b* and linked together in this way.

EYE RHYME

When words of a similar spelling make you think that they should rhyme – but don't. For instance:

> That where the ring-dove broods,
> And the badgers roll at ease
> There who once, a road through the woods.

> (Rudyard Kipling, 'The Way through the Woods')

ENJAMBMENT

Enjambment comes from the French, meaning 'to stride', and 'jambe' means leg, so you could think of striding over one line in to the next. A poet can create suspense or momentum by allowing the meaning to run on to the next line or stanza without punctuation.

> maggie and milly and molly and may
> went down to the beach(to play one day)
>
> and maggie discovered a shell that sang
> so sweetly she couldn't remember her troubles,and
>
> milly befriended a stranded star
> whose rays five languid fingers were;
>
> (e e cummings, 'maggie and milly and molly and may')

SIMILE

A comparison, normally using 'like' or 'as':

> Timothy Winters comes to school
> With eyes as wide as a football pool,
> Ears like bombs and teeth like splinters:
> A blitz of a boy is Timothy Winters.
>
> (Charles Causley, 'Timothy Winters')

METAPHOR

Metaphor is related to simile, but a metaphor insists that one thing *is* another, rather than comparing them.

> All the world's a stage,
> And all the men and women merely players:
> They have their exits and their entrances;
> And one man in his time plays many parts,
> His acts being seven ages . . .
>
> (William Shakespeare, *As you Like It*)

Here, Shakespeare tells us that the world is a stage, and then uses this notion to show us a different way of examining our lives. Metaphor can be very complex, but all of us use metaphors every day. Have you ever heard someone describe your bedroom as a 'pig-sty', or heard somebody insist that 'time is money'? If so, you already use and recognise metaphors.

HYPERBOLE

Enormous exaggeration. 'I've told you a million times.' Have you really? Or are you being hyperbolic?

LITOTES

Understatement, much used by heroes and British people. For example, after a man is shot in the leg, he might gallantly proclaim that it is 'only a scratch'. Equally, after someone is given a knighthood and wins the lottery within twenty-four hours, he might say that it had been 'not an appalling day'.

PERSONIFICATION

Giving an inanimate object or an abstract idea the characteristics of a human being. For instance, you could say of a summer's day that 'the sun smiled on us'. This cannot be literally true, since stars do not have faces or good moods.

ALLEGORY

A method of telling two stories simultaneously, one of which carries a moral or social message. For example, Aesop's *Fables* tell us the stories of talking animals, but they normally have a moral such as 'don't be greedy' or 'avoid boastfulness'. The English novelist George Orwell wrote a book called *Animal Farm*, which used talking pigs to convey a message about the Russian Revolution.

SYMBOLISM

Using one thing to represent another: a dove for peace or a red cross for medicine. Perhaps the most basic form of symbolism is a country's flag.

IDIOM

Every person, century, area and country has its own idioms, the characteristic of the speech habits of a particular group. Such figures of speech may be less understandable to outsiders. For example, someone who didn't come from the UK might be puzzled by the phrase 'chuffed to bits'; every group has a few idioms that no one else would understand. If a Victorian were to be transported into a present-day British playground, it is fair to say that he might have difficulty understanding what was being said (that might not be his first concern, however).

ASSONANCE

The repetition of identical or similar vowel sounds in neighbouring words, so for example, 'fleet feet sweep by'.

SIBILANCE

Alliteration with an 's' is called sibilance, and this can have both a sinister (an example of sibilance in itself) or tranquil effect.

The End

Index of Authors

Index of Titles

Permission Acknowledgements

Every effort has been made to trace copyright holders and obtain their permission for the use of copyright material. The publisher apologises for any errors or omissions and would be grateful if notified of any corrections that should be incorporated in future reprints or editions of this book.

The publishers gratefully acknowledge permission to reprint copyright material in this book as follows:

JOHN AGARD: 'Poetry Jump-Up' copyright © 1990 by John Agard reproduced by kind permission of John Agard c/o Caroline Sheldon Literary Agency Limited.

ALLAN AHLBERG: 'Please Mrs Butler' from *Please Mrs Butler* by Allan Ahlberg (Kestrel 1983, Puffin Books 1984) Copyright © Allan Ahlberg, 1983.

MAYA ANGELOU: 'Caged Bird' copyright © Maya Angelou 1969. Reproduced from *The Complete Collected Poems* by Maya Angelou with kind permission of Virago Press, an imprint of Little, Brown Book Group (print). 'Caged Bird', copyright © 1983 by Maya Angelou, from *Shaker, Why Don't You Sing?* By Maya Angelou. Used by permission of Random House, Inc (eBook).

W.H. AUDEN: Copyright © 1936 by W.H. Auden (Night Mail) and © 1938 by W.H. Auden (Musèe), reprinted by permission of Curtis Brown, Ltd.

HILAIRE BELLOC: 'Matilda' and 'The Frog' from *Cautionary Tales* by Hilaire Belloc reprinted by permission of Peters Fraser & Dunlop (www.petersfraserdunlop.com) on behalf of the Estate of Hilaire Belloc.

JOHN BETJEMAN: 'Hunter Trials' copyright © John Betjeman by permission of The Estate of John Betjeman.

ELIZABETH BISHOP: 'One Art' from *The Complete Poems 1927-1979* by Elizabeth Bishop. Copyright © 1979, 1983 by Alice Helen Methfessel. Reprinted by permission of Farrar, Straus and Giroux, LLC.

TIM BURTON: 'The Girl with Many Eyes' from *The Melancholy Death of Oyster Boy* © Tim Burton and reprinted with permission.

CHARLES CAUSLEY: 'Timothy Winters' from *Collected Poems* published by Macmillan and reprinted by permission of David Higham Associates Ltd.

WENDY COPE: 'Kenneth' reprinted by permission of United Agents on behalf of Wendy Cope.

E.E. CUMMINGS: 'maggie and milly and molly and may' copyright © 1956, 1984, 1991 by the Trustees for the E.E. Cummings Trust, from *Complete Poems: 1904-1962* by E.E. Cummings, edited by George J. Firmage. Used by permission of Liveright Publishing Corporation.

ROALD DAHL: 'Down Vith Children!' from *The Witches* published by Jonathan Cape Ltd and Penguin Books Ltd and reprinted by permission of David Higham Associates Ltd.

WALTER DE LA MARE: 'Silver' reprinted by permission of The Literary Trustees of Walter de la Mare and The Society of Authors as their representative.

Acknowledgements

We are grateful for all the help and advice that friends and family have given us on our merry jaunt from the kitchen table to the making of the iF Poems app to this book. In particular we would like to thank Tif Loehnis, Jenny Lord and the team at Canongate; Gina Bellman, Tim Burton, Russell Clark, Stuart Field, Paul Keegan, Linda Kelly, Natasha Lehrer, Charlotte Mitchell, Isobel Monro, Lucy Pearse, James Sherwood, Sarah Vine, Amy Waite, Maisie Lawrence, Katherine Bucknell, Rupert Walters and Samantha Weinberg; the actors who read on our iF Poems app Helena Bonham Carter, Harry Enfield, Tom Hiddleston and Bill Nighy; our husbands Mark Esiri and Sebastian Grigg; and our parents for introducing us to poetry in the first place.